Seville
and
Western Andalucia

Jerez de la Frontera

Seville
and
Western Andalucia

David Hewson

MEREHURST PRESS
LONDON

Published 1990 by Merehurst Press
Ferry House, 51-7 Lacy Road
Putney, London SW15 1PR

© Merehurst Ltd 1990

ISBN 1 85391 038 4

Designed and produced by Snap! Books
Typeset by David Hewson and Lin-Art, Ashford,
Kent, UK
Illustrations by Ann Johns
Cover illustration: detail from Alorda, 'Vista
Sevilla' reproduced by kind permission of
Arxiu MAS, Barcelona.

Maps by Sue Lawes
Printed in Great Britain by Butler and Tanner,
Frome, Somerset

Contents

Seville

Author's Preface

This is a selective, practical guide to the principal sights of western Andalucia, written with the requirements of the independent traveller in mind. It outlines a reasonably busy itinerary for a two-week tour of the area, offering you advice on what to see, where to stay, and where to eat. I have not sought to list every place of interest, since to do so would require a visit extending well beyond two weeks. Nor have I covered the many interesting sights of eastern Andalucia which you will find detailed in this book's companion guide, *Granada and Eastern Andalucia*.

The new visitor to Andalucia invariably attempts to combine east and west of the province in one grand sweep of a couple of weeks. This does scant justice to the region and will leave the unfortunate traveller weary and footsore, mentally reeling from a profusion of architectural styles and cultural mixes reflected in the great cities of Granada, Córdoba, Seville and Cádiz. If there is one piece of advice which should be paramount in briefing a visitor for this part of Europe, it is to approach the journey with patience and at a measured pace. It is impossible to see the four main cities and their surroundings in less than a month with any pleasure. If you have the time, then it is possible to combine the itinerary here with that of its sister book, performing a figure of eight across the region, the centre being in Córdoba. Those with only a fortnight to spare should avoid the customary rushed itinerary and choose to concentrate on east or west, which will allow you to delve beneath the surface somewhat more.

It is impossible to offer an opinion on which is the better. The scenery of the east is superior, with the spectacular mountains of the Sierra de Cazorla and the Alpujarra, and both Granada and Córdoba are unique cities. Yet to the west lie Seville and Cádiz and the little known delights of the Costa de la Luz, an area of charming little towns and fine seafood which the Spanish have managed to keep very much to themselves. If there is a difference, it lies in the weight of culture which the visitor will see around him. The eastern region, with its two great cities and the beautiful Renaissance town of Ubeda, offers more in the way of architecture and Moslem remains than the west. In Seville and Ronda there is much in the way of old buildings to admire, but beyond these cities the pleasures are often less demanding: tasting sherry in one of the great *bodegas* of Jerez de la Frontera, enjoying the views of the Moroccan coast from the castle walls of Tarifa, eating fresh seafood in Cádiz and El Puerto de Santa Maria, and discovering several delightful paradors, the state hotels of Spain which can rank among the most memorable places to stay in Europe. For the traveller it is a lazier region than the east, and may be approached at a more relaxed pace, with fewer worries about the opening hours of the local monuments and the possibility of vast herds of tourist coaches clogging up the streets for miles around.

The Itinerary begins in Seville. I recommend you aim to arrive in the city the evening before starting the journey. The twelfth day ends in Ayamonte, by the Portuguese border, from whence you can return to Seville for your homeward journey. At the end of each day I have suggested some worthwhile restaurants and overnight accommodation.

Travel is about discovery which is why, in the main, I do not try to instruct the reader on where to turn left and where to bear right. Most of the places visited here are not so large that an intelligent visitor cannot find his or her way around, asking directions if necessary. The only exceptions to this rule are in Seville and Ronda where, as I know from my own experience, idle, uninformed wandering can lead you to pass by worthwhile sights unknowingly. You will probably visit the great Cathedral of Seville only once in your life, and it is worth knowing, before you enter, what there is to see and where to find it.

One should also bear in mind that, wherever the journey has led, it is still Spain... and Spain is a country like no other. Opening hours, street names, and even the names of churches can and will change for no apparent reason. It is impossible to approach any part of Spain expecting it to be a well-marked and organised haven which exists to cater for foreign tourists looking for something to admire. Spain, even in some of the most popular parts, remains essentially Spanish. It is one of the country's strong points, but also one which can, on occasion, be infuriating. The knowledge of even a handful of Spanish phrases can ease these difficulties to a remarkable degree and may also transform the most unhelpful of attendants.

Introduction
to Western Andalucia

Cádiz

Andalucia is a vast province, stretching from the border of Portugal in the west to the province of Almería in the east. This itinerary covers less than a quarter of the region yet there is so much to see you will need a good two weeks to complete the journey. The route lies in an area bounded by Seville to the north, Spain's southernmost point of Tarifa to the south, and the border town of Ayamonte to the west. Seville, the country's fourth largest city and the regional capital, dominates southern Spain, culturally, socially and politically.

History

To the early explorers of the Mediterranean, the Straits of Gibraltar marked the end of civilisation, with the twin peaks on either side of the narrow channel representing the Pillars of Hercules which supported the world. Phoenicians traded with Cádiz from the earliest days, but it was the Romans who brought organisation to the region. There were important settlements at Cádiz, Italica near Seville, and at Carmona, and the latter claims to be the oldest constantly inhabited town in Europe.

After the collapse of the Roman empire came the brief rule of the Christian Visigoths of northern Europe, whose constant quarrellings paved the way for the Moslem invasion from north Africa in 711. There was an Islamic presence in southern Spain until the fall of the Kingdom of Granada in 1492, from which the region has inherited many of its most beautiful buildings.

The Moslem period was marked by conflicts between different factions and eventually degenerated into rivalries which occasionally burst into armed conflict. Seville's best known building, the Giralda tower of the Cathedral, is principally the minaret of a mosque built by the fundamentalist Almohad dynasty who invaded from north Africa in order to put down what they saw as the decadence of the then Moslem rulers. The west of Andalucia was the first area to be recaptured by Christian kings from the north. Seville fell to Ferdinand the Saint in 1248, and from this point on, the remaining Moslem leaders were, effectively, ruling vassal states on the sufferance of the Christian monarchies.

Both Seville and Cádiz prospered from the exploration and exploitation of the New World by Spanish adventurers in the 16th and 17th centuries, becoming two of the wealthiest cities in Europe. After the failure of the Armada against Britain in 1588, Spain declined as a European nation, but its sizable fleet maintained its colonial interests and continued the links with South America which are still reflected in festivals and architecture in Cádiz and Seville today. After the Battle of Trafalgar, off Cádiz, in which Nelson's fleet defeated the combined French and Spanish forces, there were popular risings against the occupation of Spain by Napoleon, the best known being in Cádiz where an independent parliament, the *Cortes*, was proclaimed. The revolt was crushed brutally, and the South American colonies took advantage of the political confusion in Spain to declare their independence.

Decades of political chaos culminated in the Civil War which began in 1936. Seville was an early stronghold of Franco's Nationalists, and an important base for their attempts to link up with right-wing forces in the north of the country. The war ended in 1939 with the defeat of the Republican forces and the fall of Barcelona, Madrid and Valencia. During the Franco years, Spain's recovery from its dire economic plight was hampered by a repressive regime which won few friends in Europe or beyond. The dictator's death in 1975 paved the way for the introduction of democracy, under the guidance of King Juan Carlos, and entry into the Common Market. Spain is now one of the fastest-growing economies in Europe, and a nation with a taste for high fashion, the luxuries of modern life, and international culture... albeit one which is often modified by the mores of the past. A young Andalucian will be as happy dancing to rock music at a beach party as he is struggling to shoulder the carriage of the Virgin in Holy Week.

Geography

The two most prominent features of western Andalucia are the plain of the Guadalquivir river, which rises in the east and flows through Córdoba and Seville to the Atlantic, and the mountain ranges that rise south of Seville and stretch to the Straits of Gibraltar. The low, flat Guadalquivir plain near

Seville is Spain's hottest region. Andalucian agriculture encompasses virtually everything modern man needs to grow. Around Jerez stand vast plains of vineyards for the sherry industry, forests of oak are harvested for cork between Ronda and Algeciras, and the Guadalquivir plain is a market garden of fruit and vegetable smallholdings.

In the mountains the most important town is the old Moslem stronghold of Ronda, and elsewhere lie scores of small *pueblos blancos*, white hill towns which are virtually untouched by modern tourism. The flat coast which runs from Tarifa to the border with Portugal at Ayamonte is known as the Costa de la Luz, the Coast of Light. The heat haze of the Mediterranean east of the Straits of Gibraltar is dispelled by the cool air coming off the Atlantic, giving clear blue skies for much of the year. It is principally an area for domestic tourism, with a string of small fishing villages overlooking secluded golden beaches. Cádiz is the most important city on the coast, and has an enchanting old town set behind sea walls on a promontory. Fishing, fruit growing and viticulture, much of it for the sherry *bodegas* of Jerez de la Frontera, el Puerto de Santa Maria, and Sanlúcar de Barrameda, are the dominant industries of the coast.

The climate in the west is varied. Seville has very hot summers and mild, occasionally wet winters. By the Atlantic and in the mountains, cool breezes make some of the hottest summer days bearable and winters are colder.

Art and Architecture

Andalucia's greatest contribution to the world of painting was made in Seville in the 17th century. The Sevillian school, which flowered and died in the space of a hundred years, produced some of Spain's greatest artists, among them Murillo, Zurbarán and Valdés Leal. All were prolific and eager for commissions, which has left Andalucia with several fine art collections, most notably in Seville and Cádiz. The Sevillian school was a mirror of the times. Seville of the 17th century was awash with riches from the New World, but also a society which was notorious for its moral decadence. It was the world of Don Juan, an allegorical tale set in Seville and, according to some, based upon one of the city's better known lotharios who, unlike the unfortunate Don, saw the error of his ways in time to placate a vengeful Creator. The story of Don Miguel de Mañara is one we shall meet later, in Seville, and it will be accompanied by a spinechilling painting by Valdés Leal which says much of the atmosphere in which the Sevillian school was created. From this mix of plague and Inquisition, spirituality and Christian love came the body of paintings which today encompasses Valdés Leal's gory horror canvases and the transcendental beauty of Murillo's saints, holy infants and Virgins.

The greatest influence on architecture has been north Africa. The brick-work curlicues of the Giralda tower and the delicate arches of the Alcázar are copied to this day. Seville's finest hotel, the grandiose Alfonso XIII is a 20th-century Moslem palace for the wealthy modern traveller. On a more mundane level, the tile and ceramic makers of Seville's Triana suburb still turn out Arabic designs for everyday home decoration and find their wares in great demand. The influence of Moslem architecture is unconscious and all pervasive, in public and private buildings large and small. At Tarifa, Spain's closest point to Africa, the very town itself is modelled on a Moroccan settlement, with narrow streets leading to the sea walls which are a carbon copy of the *souks*, or markets, to be found across the Straits of Gibraltar in most north African villages.

Western Andalucia's great musical gift to the world has been the gypsy song and dance of *flamenco* and the slower, more emotional, *cante jondo*. In the working class suburb of Triana flamenco is a way of life. Purists believe that the gypsies of Triana, who claim to have invented flamenco in the 19th century, are the leading exponents of the art in modern Spain. The sound of guitars drifts down from small apartments, heels stamp in echoing dance schools, and male voices strain for the high emotion which is the hallmark of fine flamenco. There are organised flamenco displays, for both Spanish and foreign tourists, but none can match the honesty and vigour of the impromptu performances to be found in Triana's small bars or the street festivals of the city.

The Epicure's Guide

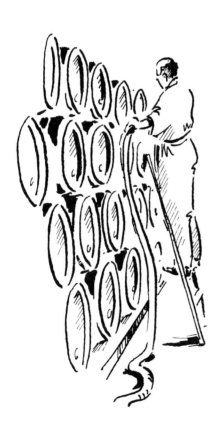

Food

With a little practice, it is hard to eat badly in modern Spain. Even in remote areas, one can rely upon the traditional fare of rural communities, *jamón serrano*, wind-dried mountain ham, one of the many good cheeses, such as *queso manchego*, spicy olives and fresh bread. In the towns, the Spaniard's love of food is generally reflected in a range of restaurants and *tapas* bars serving dishes from various regions of Spain, Galicia's famous fish specialities such as *pulpo a la gallega* (boiled octopus with paprika and oil), Castilian roast lamb, and the northern dishes of Asturias such as *fabada*, made with pork and beans. *Tapas*, the tiny titbits bought at a bar counter to accompany aperitifs, are a way of life of their own, and a few dishes of tapas can often substitute for a restaurant meal. The best, on this itinerary, are to be found in Seville and Cádiz, and each city has here a brief guide to the best tapas bars and the local specialities to be sought.

Poor restaurants exist in Spain, as they do everywhere. Those which cater primarily for tourists are rarely worth a visit. Among the worst in this category is the ghetto of cheap restaurants clustered around Seville's Cathedral which should be avoided by anyone with the faintest regard for his or her digestive system. Nor should it be assumed that a restaurant which caters solely for the Spanish must, per se, be worthwhile. The Spanish are as fond of junk food as any other nation, and some of the worst dishes I have eaten in Andalucia have been in restaurants catering for the working class Spaniard on a beach holiday. Judge a restaurant by its popularity – for the bad ones do not attract regular clientele – and the freshness of the food on display. For those with the time and the energy, it is also possible to judge many a restaurant by ordering a glass of wine and a plate of tapas while browsing through the menu.

Food and drink in Spain are no longer the bargain they once were. But it is still possible to eat well and reasonably at a variety of levels. In terms of value for money, I have no doubt that the best is to be found in the most expensive restaurants. Menus of the quality of Seville's Oriza and El Puerto's Alboronia are dear in Spanish terms, but the food can stand comparison with the best London and New York restaurants and may be only half what one would therefore expect to pay. Those on a budget are less well served. There is a dearth of good, inexpensive cafés. The best are those catering for local workers and selling *platos combinados*, fixed price plates of ham and eggs, sausages, pork chops and the inevitable chips. The *menu del dia* is a fixed price, three-course menu including bread and wine which *can* be a bargain provided it is not in a tourist den. Wherever you eat, it is worth remembering that you will get what you pay for. A *menu del dia* offering *gazpacho, paella*, and a steak for under 1,000 pesetas is unlikely to be memorable, except for all the wrong reasons.

There is a thoroughly confusing official system of restaurant ratings based upon the award of one to three forks. The criterion is one of decor and setting, not standard of food. Several of the best restaurants in Andalucia fail to achieve a three fork rating simply because of their location. The pricing policies of establishments may also cause confusion. Modest and popular local restaurants and *bodegas* will frequently have a daily menu of medium-priced dishes with a small number of luxury specialities costing four or five times the price of a normal meal. Baby eels, *angulas*, all kinds of prawn, lobster and crab, and the best *jamón* can be very expensive indeed, even at the counter of a neighbourhood bar which also serves cheap tapas. The moral is a simple one: always ask the price of something before ordering it. Simply pointing to the display behind the bar can lead to nasty shocks, more through misunderstandings rather than any dishonesty on the part of the waiter. Expensive fish and shellfish are often sold by weight at the prevailing market prices.

Cuisine is so localised in Spain that it is hard to generalise about any particular region. In western Andalucia, as well as the many regional restaurants which abound, you will encounter three different schools of Andalucian cuisine. The most defined is that of the coast, at its best in the restaurants of Cádiz. Here the fish of the Atlantic, more tasty than their Mediterranean cousins, dominate the menu. Tiny anchovies, fresh squid, cuttlefish, and handsome sea bream are fried to a dry crispness or turned into the local fish soup, *sopa al cuarta de hora*. *Bacalao* (salt cod) and *huevos aliñadas* (cold cod roe in vinegar) appear in salads with chopped peppers, tomatoes and onion. This reliance on Atlantic fish runs the length of the coast, from Tarifa to the Portuguese border, with the local catches dictating the dominant specialities, tuna in the south, skate in the north.

The contrast with the food of the mountains around Ronda could hardly be greater. Here pork, game, vegetables and eggs have sustained communities which, until the arrival of the car, were days away from the coast. Ham, a wide variety of sausages, partridge, and *revueltos*, lightly scrambled eggs with vegetables such as wild asparagus, form some of the best dishes. A common accompaniment to eggs and sausage is *migas*, breadcrumbs fried in oil with garlic. The food of the mountains is unsophisticated and largely unchanged by modern culinary trends.

Finally, Seville is a thriving culinary city, busily absorbing outside influences while simultaneously maintaining its own traditions. *Pato sevillana*, duck casseroled with olives, and *rabo de toro*, oxtail casserole, are among the specialities of the city. Dishes from all the neighbouring parts of Andalucia are readily imported, particularly those of Jerez which involve cooking chicken, kidneys and other meat in sherry or sherry vinegar.

Modern Spanish cooking, which combines nouvelle cuisine with the fish, shellfish and vegetables of Spain, is fashionable in Seville, with new restaurants opening almost monthly. Brief cooking and an absence of heavy, fried ingredients are the only two common themes in this cuisine; the rest is determined by the skill and inventiveness of the chef. The large prawns of Sanlúcar de Barrameda have a fame which extends beyond Jerez to Seville where you will find them served, at a price, in shellfish bars.

Spanish desserts are normally very sweet, using masses of sugar and honey. Those without a sweet tooth may prefer a plate of cheese, or fresh fruit, a course which is increasingly followed by calorie-conscious Spanish diners.

Flan is a crème caramel found everywhere, and usually mass-produced. *Crema Catalana* is a delicious custard often scorched with a crust of burnt sugar before serving. Various kinds of frozen cake, *tarta helada*, will be found in a cabinet in many restaurants, along with good Minorcan fruit ice creams packed into frozen oranges, lemons and pineapples. *Leche frita*, fried milk, is a sweet, fried custard, and *natillas* a spiced custard served with biscuits. *Arroz con leche* is nothing more than a spiced rice pudding, while the ubiquitous *tocine del cielo* is a rather sickly – to me at least – concoction of custard and caramel. More healthy fare is usually available, such as fresh fruit or *nueces con nata*, a variety of nuts with dried fruit and cream.

Wine and Drinks

This is sherry country. *Fino*, dry sherry from Jerez de la Frontera and El Puerto de Santa Maria, or *manzanilla*, a close relation from Sanlúcar de la Barrameda, are drunk as aperitifs and as white table wine, with food. A simple request for *vino* will usually be misheard as *fino* and result in a glass of dry sherry. White table wine is best described as *vino blanco* to guarantee that you do not get sherry; red is *vino tinto*. There is greater detail on the four principal kinds of sherry in the section on Jerez, the home of the great sherry *bodegas* (see pp. 96-7).

Table wine may come from anywhere in Spain, local vineyards, those of larger regions such as Valdepeñas or Penedes, or the best known wine area, Rioja. Rioja whites and reds are generally matured in oak and formidable in strength and character. While this may produce hearty reds which cry out for roast beef to accompany them, it is somewhat heavy-handed on the whites. An exception is the ubiquitous Monopole, to my mind a rather thin white with nothing to justify its high price tag, but a wine, nevertheless, which seems to have penetrated everywhere. Local table wines may be more suited to hot summer weather. A popular drink in hot weather is *tinto de verano*, the 'red of summer' which is nothing more than red wine mixed with soda water or the popular soft drink *La Casera*, served with ice.

The Spanish are only just beginning to experiment with adapting viticulture to changing modern tastes, and several lighter, more sophisticated wines are coming onto the market at the time of writing. They are unlikely to be found outside the lists of the best, modern restaurants; for the old standards like Seville's Burladero, the heart of the matter is a list of fine old reds, principally from Rioja, with a smattering of heavy whites on the side. Anyone wishing to cultivate a serious interest in Spanish wine – a fast-changing subject – would be advised to subscribe to the excellent English magazine *LookOut*, published monthly in Spain, which carries an informed and informative wine column (see Bibliography).

If an Andalucian does not drink sherry with his plate of seafood, then he will doubtless buy a glass of beer, *cerveza*. Spanish beer is the usual gassy lager found elsewhere in southern Europe. An occasional alternative is mineral water, *agua mineral*, drunk plain, *sin gas*, or carbonated, *con gas*.

The sherry houses of Jerez use their grape output to produce several strengths and qualities of brandy. EEC rules prevent them calling the results *coñac*, though it is still known as such in every bar and restaurant. The best, such as those from the Terry, Osborne and Byass houses, arc smooth and palatable; cheaper brandies are firewater.

Spanish coffee is normally served black, *solo*, in small cups like Italian espresso. *Cafe con leche* is *solo* mixed with hot milk. Instant coffee is always called *Nescafé*. *Té*, tea, is usually served with lemon, *con limón*. The adventurous may come across one curiosity here when ordering the sherry of Sanlúcar, *manzanilla*. This is also the name of a herbal tea infusion; if the waiter seems confused, make sure that you emphasise whether you want tea or something a little stronger.

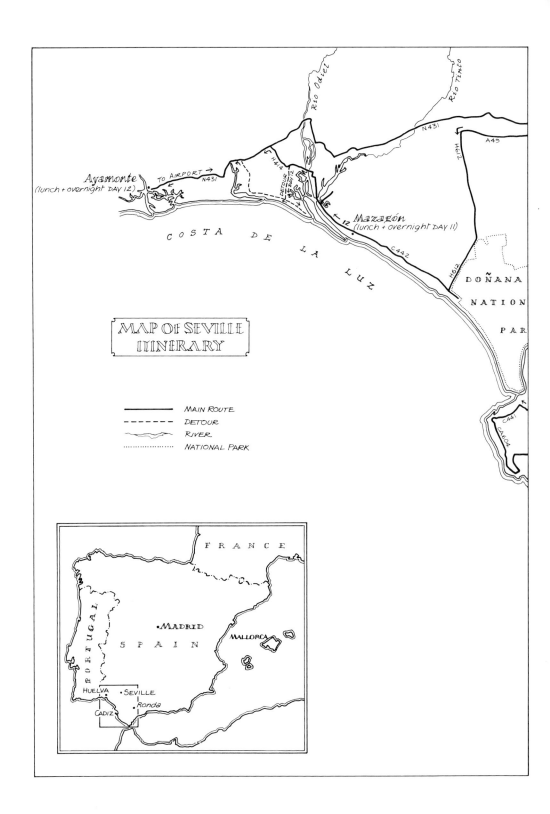

MAP OF SEVILLE
ITINERARY

Ayamonte
(lunch + overnight DAY 12)

Mazagón
(lunch + overnight DAY 11)

COSTA   DE   LA   LUZ

TO AIRPORT →

N431

Rio Odiel

Rio Tinto

N431

A49

H414

C442

H612

DOÑANA

NATION

PAR

CA441

CA604

—————— MAIN ROUTE
- - - - - DETOUR
~~~~~~~~ RIVER
········· NATIONAL PARK

FRANCE

MADRID

MALLORCA

SPAIN

PORTUGAL

HUELVA

SEVILLE

Ronda

CADIZ

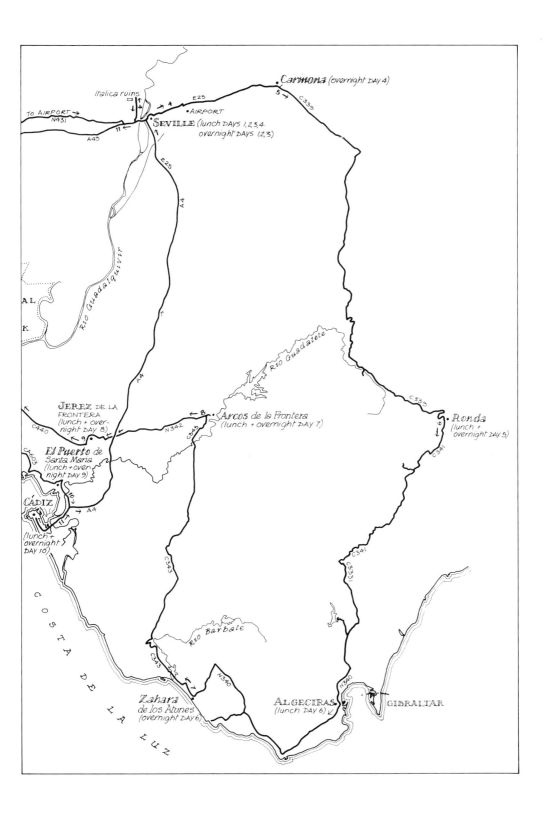

Handy Tips

HOW TO GET THERE FROM THE UK
The Itinerary begins and ends in Seville.

By Air — There are regular, in most cases daily, flights from major European cities to Seville. Some charter flights are available from the UK, but schedule airline prices, particularly those from the Spanish state airline Iberia, are often very competitive with inclusive car hire. Schedule and charter flights to Gibraltar would enable the traveller to take up this itinerary, beginning at Day 6 in Zahara de los Atunes, which is an hour's drive from the Rock. Car hire in Gibraltar is generally more expensive than in Spain. The busy and popular entry airport of Málaga is about three hours drive from Ronda. Given the pressure on Spanish air space, it makes sense, whenever possible, to travel midweek and not at weekends.

By Car — The fastest route recommended by the AA is to enter Spain by San Sebastián and travel to Seville via Burgos, and Madrid, then taking the fast NIV to Seville via Valdepeñas and Córdoba. The AA will produce for members excellent individual itineraries, outlining routes to Spain from the Channel ports which take into account roadworks, if contacted at least two weeks before departure. In general, the recommended route south from Calais and Boulogne skirts Paris on the Boulevard Périphérique, leaving by the A10 south through Tours and Bordeaux. It is advisable to check on roadworks and other possible delays in advance. Spain is currently suffering a rash of thefts from cars. Wherever possible park in a secure garage in large cities, and never leave possessions on view.

WHEN TO GO
The most pleasant time to visit Andalucia is in May or early June, September, or early October. The plain around Seville is Spain's hottest region, with temperatures in summer regularly in the 90s for the best part

of the day. This is not a problem if you have an air-conditioned hotel room and observe the siesta. On the Atlantic coast, summer days are cooler, often with a pleasant breeze. Winters are normally mild and relatively dry. The peak of the tourist season is Holy Week, when hotel bookings are essential and all facilities overstretched.

FESTIVALS AND OTHER EVENTS

Semana Santa in Seville is Spain's most famous festival, a week of passionate religious processions followed by an enormous fair over the Easter week-end in the Maria Luisa park. Hotel rooms are booked for years in advance. If you want to visit the city during Holy Week, contact one of the major travel agencies, such as Thomas Cook, who will usually have block book-ings of rooms at the major hotels. No-one sleeps during *Semana Santa* and events may be lost on anyone who does not have some grasp of Spanish, so do not expect a conventional, relaxing holiday. Smaller, but equally noisy, Holy Week celebrations take place in most cities and towns throughout Andalucia. There are also fairs for *Corpus Christi* and a bewildering number of saints' days. While many have religious origins, the modern *feria* is prin-cipally a secular event, with music, dancing and fairground stalls active throughout the night.

BANKS

Banks are open from 9am to 2am on weekdays and 9am to 1pm on Saturdays. Eurocheques, backed by a guarantee card, are commonly accepted in hotels, restaurants and shops. Many UK cashcards can now be used in 24-hour Spanish cash dispenser machines though prior arrange-ments may need to be made with the user's bank.

SHOPPING

The majority of shops creak into life around 9.30am and shut again between 1pm and 2pm, reopening around 4.30pm until about 8pm.

MONUMENTS AND MUSEUMS

Normal opening hours are from 10am to 1.30pm and 4.30pm to 6.30pm. Some extend the evening closing time until 8pm.

DRIVING

The speed limits are: 60km/h (37mph) in built-up areas, 100km/h (62mph) on main roads, 120km/h (74mph) on motorways, and 90km/h

(56mph) on other roads. Car hire from international companies tends to be around 30 per cent more expensive than from domestic car hire firms.

LANGUAGE

Andalucians speak Castilian – that is, Spanish – with a local accent. The most noticeable regional characteristic is to pronounce 'c' as a soft 's' instead of 'th': in other words *gracias* is pronounced 'gra*s*ias' not 'gra*th*ias' as it is elsewhere in Spain.

KEY TO ITINERARY

Ratings are an indication of the cost of a room or meal, not a judgement on the quality of the establishment, all of which are good within their price range.

**	Reasonable	****	Expensive
***	Average	*****	Very expensive

To follow the Itinerary I recommend you use Michelin Map Spanish series no. 446. Within the text there is a general map of the area on pp. 22-3, and detailed routes as follows:

Days 1-5, p. 59   Day 11, p.119
Days 6-8, p. 75   Day 12, p.128
Days 9-10, p.101

At the beginning of each day in the Itinerary there is a summary of the day's route and grid references of the places visited. Grid references are latitude first, then longitude (i.e. reading from the perimeter of the map, the vertical number then the horizontal). Each square represents 20'.

The Itinerary

La Giralda, Seville

DAY 1

Seville – the Cathedral and Alcázar. A full day on foot spent in the quarter of the city's most famous sights, the Cathedral and the fortress of the Christian king Pedro the Cruel.

Overnight in Seville.

Map reference
Seville   37° 25´N 5° 58´W

Seville

Arrive in Seville.

It is probably simpler if you arrive in Seville the evening before beginning the itinerary in order to devote the maximum amount of time to exploring the city.

Seville is a large and lively place which may swamp the first-time visitor with a wealth of sights, sounds and emotions. It is a rich course for anyone to digest, and as such should be taken at a measured pace. The temptation to cram as many sights as possible into one day can only lead to exhaustion and confusion, which is why the walks outlined here are relatively leisurely.

It is impossible to see all this great city in three days, but my itinerary covers the main tourist sights. If you are to enjoy your visit, a degree of forethought and a certain frame of mind are required. Parts of the city are largely given over to the tourist trade, and if you stay or eat there you must expect to be treated in the rather cursory fashion meted out to tourists in most modern cities. The well-known Barrio de Santa Cruz, while still worth visiting, virtually lives off tourism these days, with all that that means. Yet it remains a Spanish barrio, and if you stay there you must expect to keep Spanish hours. For those who like to retire to bed before midnight, this could be the worst of all possible worlds.

During the summer, Seville boils, with daytime temperatures regularly approaching 100°F (38°C). There is a conventional wisdom which urges you to avoid the place at this time. Personally, I prefer it... on condition that I have an air-conditioned room in a hotel so situated that sleep after midnight is not impossible, such as the Alfonso or the Inglaterra. This is the city in which to spoil yourself on a good hotel, particularly in summer when the average Sevilliano thinks that the evening begins at midnight.

A visit to Seville can begin in only one place, under the shadow of its most famous landmark, the Giralda belltower of the Cathedral. The siesta, which is largely observed with almost religious devotion, always looms large in any planned itinerary here. It is, to my mind, impossible to try to cram both the Cathedral, the largest of its kind in the world, and the neighbouring palace of the Alcázar into a morning and gain much from the experience. My advice is to enter the Cathedral as soon as possible after it opens at 10.30am, to visit the Archive of the Indies next door before lunch, and

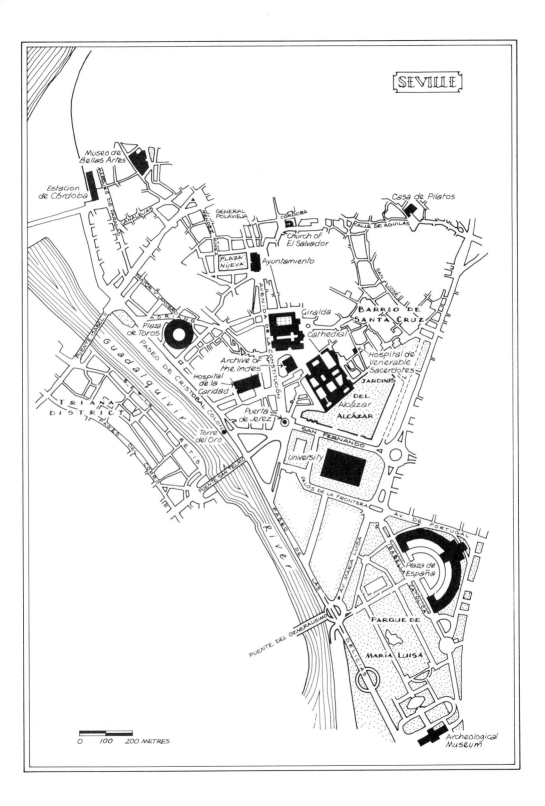

SEVILLE

Museo de Bellos Artes

Estacion de Córdoba

MARQUES DE PARADAS

CANALEJAS

MENDEZ NUÑEZ

GENERAL POLAVIEJA

CORDOBA

Casa de Pilatos

CALLE DE AGUILAS

Church of El Salvador

PLAZA NUEVA

Ayuntamiento

SAN JOSÉ

SAN LUIS

ADRIANO

Plaza de Toros

PUENTE ISABEL II

PASTOR Y LANDERO

AVENIDA DE LA CONSTITUCIÓN

Giralda

BARRIO DE SANTA CRUZ

Cathedral

Archive of the Indes

Hospital de Venerable Sacerdotes

Guadalquivir

BAILEN

PASEO DE CRISTOBAL COLON

Hospital de la Caridad

JARDINES

DEL Alcázar

ALCÁZAR

T R I A N A   D I S T R I C T

BETIS

PASEO DEL CORRO

Puerta de Jerez

Torre del Oro

SAN FERNANDO

University

PUENTE SAN TELMO

PALOS DE LA FRONTERA

River

PASEO DE LAS

AV. DE PORTUGAL

AV. MARIA LUISA

ISABEL CATÓLICA

DELICIAS

Plaza de España

PUENTE DEL GENERALISIMO

PARQUE DE

MARÍA LUISA

0   100   200 METRES

Archeological Museum

then to visit the Alcázar in the afternoon, as soon as possible after 3pm when it opens its doors (closing them again at 5.30pm).

The Cathedral

The vast Cathedral is the largest Gothic place of worship in the world; the only Christian churches which are larger are St Peter's in Rome and St Paul's in London. Yet its most famous element, the Giralda, is not Christian in origin at all, but a minaret dating from the 12th century when Seville was ruled by a sect of fanatical North Africans known as the Almohads. The Moslem tower rises for 250 feet and is then topped by a later Christian addition of a belltower. The two styles mix well, and the Giralda makes a recognisable landmark from many different angles, during the day and at night when it and the Cathedral are illuminated with great skill.

Before entering the Cathedral by the south gate used for tourists it is worth walking around the outside to appreciate both its bulk and the variety of styles which it incorporates. From the Giralda walking anticlockwise, you pass three horseshoe arches of obvious Moslem origin then turn the corner to see, halfway down the west wall, an ornate Arabic gate known as the Puerta del Pardón, similar to the gate of the same name at Córdoba's famous mosque-cum-cathedral, the Mezquita. Restoration work blocks some of the view of this highly decorated gateway into the original patio of the mosque that preceded the Cathedral. But one can still see the features which typify this style of Moslem architecture, which is also commonly reflected in Córdoba and Granada. There are the lines of Arabic script which serve both as decorative designs and as sayings from religious documents, and the intricate stucco work in complex geometric patterns. Later Christian additions and statues sit rather uneasily in these surroundings.

The west side of the Cathedral runs alongside the busy main road of the Avenida de la Constitución and possesses three entrances, all of them affected by the grime of modern city life. The Puerta de San Miguel, the last when walking anticlockwise, is judged to be the best and contains some terracotta work notable for its now odd coloration. Around the corner once more and you face the rich 19th-century south gate which lies opposite the two-storey square Archive of the Indies, once an exchange building. To the left is the Alcázar, with horse carriages vying for custom in the space between. It is a pleasant, unhurried corner of this hectic city.

On entering the Cathedral you will immediately see positive proof of its importance in the scheme of Spanish affairs. A coffin faces the visitor, borne aloft by four figures representing Aragon, Castile, Navarre, and Leon, the four Spanish kingdoms. It contains the remains of Christopher Columbus, whose discovery of the New World, and the conquests to which that led, enriched Spain in general and Seville in particular. Above the tomb is an enormous painting of St Christopher; the two make for a spectacular entrance. Columbus was buried in Havana, one of the many Spanish colonies, and his remains were brought to Seville in 1899 when it was apparent that the age of the empire was on the wane.

The vastness of the interior beckons on either side, but, ignoring it and, as much as one possibly can, the towering gold altar in the centre to the right, walk ahead, towards the door into the Patio de los Naranjos which, on sunny days, will normally be left open, throwing a bright beam of sunlight into the nave. In this outdoor courtyard, with its manicured orange trees, the Moslems of Seville performed their ritual ablutions before going to worship in the mosque. For the Christians who followed it became a patio for meetings and oratory.

Return to the nave and turn immediately left, towards another door which is usually open. This leads into the base of the Giralda itself, and a broad, gentle ramp which ascends the belltower, affording a memorable panorama of the city. The climb of close to 300 feet is made less strenuous by the use of a ramp instead of steps, and the Giralda is so sturdy that the effort should not deter those who normally have no head for heights. The inside of the tower has been restored relatively recently, and one must accept the word of the reference books that Roman masonry supports the lowest portions. It would have been eminently sensible of the Almohads to have plundered Roman buildings for stone, since the Seville area was an important settlement and the birthplace of the emperors Hadrian and Trajan, the latter's name being recalled in the modern suburb of Triana.

After these two excursions comes the Cathedral proper. Returning from the Giralda, turn sharp left to face the splendour of the Royal Chapel. The body of the king and saint Ferdinand III, who captured Seville for the Christian cause in 1248, lies in the ornate silver casket in front of the altar. Above him is the figure of the Virgen de los Reyes which was carried ceremoniously with Ferdinand's party throughout his campaigns. It is to the

Virgin that these quiet figures with bowed heads are praying, not to the saintly Ferdinand, for the cult of the Virgin, with its pre-Christian origins, is still strong in Spain.

Leaving the chapel you face the rear of the Chapel of the High Altar, fashioned as a house front and bearing paintings. The chapel contains the golden altar seen when crossing from Columbus's tomb to the Patio de los Naranjos. Gilt panels representing religious scenes tower to more than 70 feet above the floor with a breadth of some 60 feet. It is one of the world's great works of church art. The iron screen or *reja* around the altar, often ignored for the more colourful *retablo,* is a fine example of an art confined to Spain. It is the wood here, in the form of the stalls, which is most impressive, even at a distance. Visitors are barred from entering the choir in order to protect the woodwork.

Various chapels run around the exterior of the Cathedral but few would interest the casual visitor. There are two exceptions. In the north west corner is the Baptistry Chapel which contains Murillo's Vision of Saint Anthony of Padua. This was the subject of great intrigue in 1875 when a thief removed the well executed saint and left behind the rather less attractive cherubs above him. The stolen portion was recovered from an auction in New York and returned to Seville where restorers sealed it back onto the canvas.

On the southern side of the choir is the small Chapel of the Immaculate Conception. This contains another Virgin popular with the locals. It is the work of the great Sevillian artist Montañes, and one can see why the expressive gaze of the figure has captured so many admirers.

The final portion of the Cathedral remaining to be seen lies in the three halls at the south east corner, beyond the tomb of Columbus. These contain the Cathedral treasures and works of art. The former include the usual collection of plate expected of a wealthy Spanish city, and some of it is not as overblown as it might be. There are works by most of the best-known Andalucian artists, including Murillo, Pedro de Campana, Valdés Leal, Montañes, and Zurbarán. The principal hall is the Sacristia Mayor, a rich Renaissance room fit for such paintings. The circular chapterhouse contains works by Murillo. It is reached by the Sala de Ornamentos which contains a colourful, if ill-explained, collection of old religious vestments.

Archive of the Indies

At this point, the visitor will have seen all the major sights of the Cathedral
– closures for restoration willing, of course. If there is time before lunch,
an interesting 30 minutes may be spent in the Archive of the Indies, which
offers free entrance to all on condition that one signs in like a genuine academic researcher. This is a true archive, with rare documents stored in
neat files along the walls. But a number of the most interesting are on display, and a few copies of very rare items. So one may see the signature of
the great Columbus, a few hundred feet from where his body lies, plans for
the defence of colonies in Peru and Mexico, and drawings of the machin-
ery used by the early colonists. A plaque records that it was in this building,
in 1660, that an Academy of Arts.was established, its president being the
famous Murillo.

Lunch in Seville.

The Royal Alcázar is one of the most important *mudéjar* palaces – the term
denotes work carried out by Moslem craftsmen under Christian rule, and
the ornate style has come to be representative of Andalucia itself. The
Alcázar is not so large or varied as Granada's Alhambra, but there are portions where the workmanship exceeds anything of its kind remaining in
modern Spain. The early palace was built for the notorious Christian king
Pedro the Cruel in the 14th century, and added to, in Renaissance style, by
Charles V in the 16th century. To the right, on entering, is the commerce
house where expeditions to the New World were planned by the Christian
monarchs. There is a famous painting, the Virgen de los Navegantes, which
depicts the ever present Virgin sheltering sailors and their vessels under-
neath her cloak.

The original palace of Pedro is entered through a magnificent doorway
reminiscent of Granada's Alhambra, with its fantastic stucco patterns. A
line of blue and white tiles represents a Moslem prayer, an odd thing to
have over the palace of a Christian king you may think. Many of the craftsmen who worked on the building came from Granada, at that time a vassal,
Moslem state of Christian Seville.

Inside, the palace is rectangular with a series of rooms around the central
courtyard of the Patio de las Doncellas. The greatest chamber is the Salon

de Embajadores, which lies to the right as one enters. There is a wealth of colour, in tiles, gilt and painted stucco, reaching to the cupola which crowns the chamber. The final section of the Alcázar, the Gothic Palace of Charles V, lies next door; you must leave the *mudéjar* palace to reach it. A series of lively tapestries recording the king's expedition to Tunis line the walls of the first chamber from which one can deduce, among other things, that the standard travelling inventory of the Spanish army of the time included not only cows and sheep but ostriches too. Since the artist responsible went along with the expedition, like a modern war photographer, presumably this is no exaggeration.

The palace leads into the extensive gardens of the Alcázar, past a fountain of dubious taste. There is a small, pretty pavilion built for Charles, and the gardens are, in the main, well tended and generously stocked. Roses, eucalyptus and jasmine are but a few of the scents which drift around the lazy afternoon air.

Overnight in Seville.

ACCOMMODATION

Seville has a wide variety of hotels, with clientele ranging from back-packing students to expense account businessmen. The city is busy throughout the year, making reservations advisable. It is virtually impossible for an individual to book a room in a major hotel during Holy Week. Contact a large travel agent chain to make reservations for this hectic period.

Alfonso XIII
San Fernando 2
Seville
Tel: 222850

A mock *mudéjar* palace close to the river in the centre of the city, the
Alfonso is, without question, *the* place to stay in Seville. There is a wide
range of rooms, from singles for passing businessmen to suites for film
stars and the very wealthy. Mere mortals can wander into the bar or
restaurant and star spot; personally, I am not sure the Alfonso is quite as
good as it thinks it is, but one would be hard pressed to find its like anywhere else in the world.

Open all year
Rooms: 149
Facilities: outdoor pool, terrace
Credit cards: American Express, Diner's Club, Eurocard, Visa
Rating *****

Los Lebreros
Luis Morales 2
Seville
Tel: 579400

Modern American-style hotel with some of the most comfortable rooms in
Seville, a cab ride from the centre of the city. Popular with expense
account businessmen; staff tend to look down on mere tourists.

Open all year
Rooms: 439
Facilities: outdoor pool, nightclub, shopping mall
Credit cards: American Express, Diner's Club, Eurocard, Visa
Rating *****

Inglaterra
Pl. Nueva 7
Seville
Tel: 224970

Inglaterra contd

The author's personal choice, the Inglaterra is well situated in the centre of the city, with friendly, helpful staff always ready to offer advice and book rooms for remaining parts of the journey. Rooms are comfortable, with air conditioning, rather than luxurious, and the hotel is exceptionally quiet considering its central location.

Open all year
Rooms: 120
Credit cards: American Express, Diner's Club, Eurocard, Visa
Rating ***

Doña Maria
Don Remondo 19
Seville
Tel: 224990

Elegant, comfortable hotel very close to the Giralda, and consequently right in the middle of the tourist quarter. No garage.

Open all year
Rooms: 61
Facilities: outdoor pool, terrace
Credit cards: American Express, Diner's Club, Visa
Rating ***

Bécquer
Reyes Católicos 4
Seville
Tel: 228900

Popular, reasonably-priced tourist hotel on a busy avenue between the Plaza Nueva and the Museo des Bellas Artes. Some rooms suffer from traffic noise, but the Bécquer has won many regular visitors in recent years.

Open all year
Rooms: 126
Credit cards: American Express, Diner's Club, Eurocard, Visa
Rating **

Murillo
Lope de Rueda 9
Seville
Tel: 216095

Characterful budget accommodation in the heart of the Barrio de Santa Cruz. The hotel is somewhat eccentrically decorated, rooms are functional, but it has a certain dog-eared charm and is well-placed for the city centre. As with anywhere in the Barrio, noise from neighbouring properties can be a problem. No garage, and can only be reached by a pedestrian alleyway from the Murillo gardens. Ask the management to recommend a private parking place; under no circumstances should private cars be left in the streets near the Barrio.

Open all year
Rooms: 61
Credit cards: American Express, Diner's Club, Eurocard, Visa
Rating **

EATING OUT

For restaurants, see pp. 47-9 and tapas, see pp. 56-8.

SEVILLE: USEFUL INFORMATION	
Tourist office:	Costurero de la Reina
	Paseo de las Delicias
	Tel: 234465
Population:	685,833
Facilities:	international airport, bullring, golf

39

Gardens of the Alcázar, Seville

DAY 2

A walk around central Seville, visiting the Arabic Torre del Oro, the Archeological Museum, the Hospital de la Caridad, which has connections with the story of Don Juan, and the Plaza de Toros.

Overnight in Seville.

Map reference
Seville   37° 25´N 5° 58´W

Breakfast in Seville.

After the Giralda, the best known landmark of Seville is the Torre del Oro, the 'tower of gold' which stands on the riverfront by the busy Paseo de Cristóbal Colón. It makes an excellent starting point for a walking tour of the central city. The tower was part of the Moslem fortifications of Seville. A chain could be swung from the 12-sided building to a similar guard post on the far side of the river to hamper attacking vessels, while a wall linked the tower to the original Alcázar. Today the Torre stands alone, along a broad riverside promenade which houses fairs and cafés with views over the Guadalquivir to Triana.

It is along here that the locals take their evening stroll before deciding where to eat, not in the Barrio de Santa Cruz which is almost depopulated apart from tourists. From here virtually all the main sights of the central city are within easy walking distance.

In the popular mind Seville is most often associated with two figures who never lived: the gypsy Carmen and the libertine Don Juan. Both are characters from the pages of fiction who became yet more famous on the opera stage. The tourist coaches still point out the Fabrica de Tabacos, the tobacco factory, as 'the place where Carmen worked', and one can still see lively young girls leaving through its gates, though they are much more likely to be carrying academic books than carnations. The building is now the University and may be found by walking across the square of the Puerta de Jerez and past the luxurious Alfonso XIII hotel.

It looks nothing like a tobacco factory, this being Seville, and resembles more a military academy, with moats and sentry posts. Tobacco was, of course, a valuable commodity in the early part of the 18th century, and the girls upon whom Carmen was based were searched minutely to ensure that they did not smuggle any out of the building. Even so, it is hard to explain the military aloofness, though, as one will see later, not far away lies an artillery academy which looks very much like a university.

Seville loves Carmen, her vivid personality, her music, her whole being. More than this, everyone knows someone upon whom the very character might have been based. That she was created by a French author and made immortal by a composer of similar nationality is, of course, irrelevant;

Carmen is the spirit of Seville, and Seville is the spirit of Carmen (I give you this well-tested sequence of dialogue now so that you may be familiar with it when it crops up).

Turning right at the end of San Fernando you come to the Parque de María Luisa, as pleasant a public park as one will encounter anywhere in Spain, with fragrant gardens, shady corners, and quiet roads from which the motor car is banned. If you must have a ride in a horse carriage, then let it be here, for the roar of traffic is somewhat distant and horse drawn transport loses something when it is surrounded by tourist coaches belching diesel. On the city side of the park stands the Plaza de España, probably the most photographed part of Seville after the Giralda. There is a small canal on which rowing boats may be hired and, behind it, the grandiose building erected for the 1929 Ibero-American exhibition. Little bridges cross the canal in the Plaza and it is a place to which Sevillian families flock, mostly at weekends, clutching bags of food which are consumed amid much chatter on the park benches.

Archeological Museum

At the far end of the park stands the Archeological Museum, often neglected by visitors. The Roman collection is particularly rich and well displayed, with roomy halls which can accommodate with ease the vast statues and columns recovered from Italica. The collection of mosaics includes several beautiful examples, astonishingly intact. The museum is closed Mondays and on other days will only open its doors between 10am and 2pm (presumably as a sign of academic seriousness in order to prove that it is no mere masonry collection).

Outside the museum, near the road, is a small patio, with a suitable statue, dedicated to white doves. The birds dutifully man the place 24 hours a day and will descend upon anyone with a hint of a food about him, posing until the last frame of film or peanut has disappeared. Trafalgar Square's more mundanely dressed pigeons, who perform similar tricks, look positively scruffy by comparison, and there would be no danger of anyone describing Seville's gleaming white birds with the words once used by a member of the House of Lords of their London counterparts: 'rats with wings'.

I have outlined this section of the itinerary as one which will occupy the morning, making a break for lunch immediately after the museum visit. There are a handful of cafés in the park – the Restaurant Chile serves a very decent *pinchito* – or for something more substantial you could walk back to the restaurants behind the Torre del Oro. It is, in any case, in the latter area that you will find traces of that other great fictional personality of Seville, the sensualist Don Juan, who has come to a sticky end at the hands of Molière and Mozart, but made his initial appointment with Hades in a 17th-century play by Tirso de Molina, once a civil servant in the building which now houses the Museo de Bellas Artes.

Hospital de la Caridad

Walking towards the bullring from the Torre del Oro one sees two buildings behind a small public garden. The larger, to the left, is the artillery academy; the second is the Hospital de la Caridad, a home for the elderly and the incapacitated. The academy is still occupied by the military and has no part in the Don Juan tale, although, unlike most working army buildings, it is older than Juan and the adjoining building, dating from the 16th century. It is worth looking into the public garden before visiting the Hospital; in addition to a few of its residents taking the sun, you will find the statue of a man holding a dying beggar in his arms, and it is this charitable fellow, Don Miguel de Mañara, that Seville would have you believe is the original for the character. The link is one I have seen repeated as recently as 1988 in a Sevillian newspaper, although there is hard evidence that Mañara was either unborn or only a few years old when the play was written. None of this is believed in Seville, which happily continues to recount the tale of a licentious young noble who is turned to charitable deeds by a supernatural event. There is no agreement on precisely what that event was, but it is illuminating that one tale has Mañara confronting a woman he desires only to find that behind her veil lies a skull. This is remarkably similar to the experience of another libertine turned cleric, Ramon Llull of Mallorca, who similarly turned to God when the object of *his* desire revealed a breast gnawed by cancer, and all this a good two centuries earlier. As usual, the traveller in Spain should treat all such tales as apocryphal, preferably until one sees a written affidavit from one of the parties concerned, and Mañara, though a prolific essayist, never left that.

So, having wiped from the mind any idea that Don Juan and Mañara might be connected, buy a ticket and enter the little Hospital chapel... to find a scene which would fit happily in any account of the Don Juan tale ever produced. It is a gleaming baroque interior of the kind only a rich society could muster, and Seville in the 17th century was at its richest... and consequently most decadent. There is one truly great painting, Murillo's depiction of St Elizabeth treating a boy with ringworm and admired by a group of paupers suffering from a variety of afflictions. Its image of pure charity for the impoverished reflects the Hospital's work over the centuries, a task still continuing today.

Two other paintings which face each other across the chapel are more in keeping with the Don Juan theme, however. They are the work of Valdés Leal, a member of the Sevillian school along with Murillo, and bring to mind the final scene of the story, when the unrepentant Juan is dragged to eternal torment in Hell. A skeleton cackles at human vanity, a bishop and a grand knight rot in their tombs, their riches mouldering beside them. They are the product of a society obsessed with the briefness of life and the role of God in an age of plague and decadence, unmistakably the product of 17th-century Seville. While Mañara may not have been the role model for Juan, he must have known plenty of men who could have played the part. Outside in the patio, which is light and welcome after the horrors of Valdés Leal, there is an interesting series of tiles depicting Biblical scenes, among them a lively Jonah and the Whale.

The bullring

Beyond the artillery academy lies the bullring, the Plaza de Toros. It is, of course, a grand building and enormously popular, but there is a better ring to visit later at Ronda where the modern style of bullfighting began. Bullfighting is a complex subject, deeply rooted in the Spanish character. The foreigner will be little better equipped to understand it even after buying tickets and sitting through the fights, for it is a technical, social and emotional ritual which cannot be understood in a day.

If the matador is on poor form, it is not an event for the squeamish, nor can anyone doubt that, by the lights of Anglo-Saxon customs, it is cruel. This is not 'sport'; only the matador can win or lose, the bull will die whatever happens in the ring. The Spaniard sees none of this apparent cruelty; only a brave man and, with luck, a brave bull which is bred to die. It will do so with more dignity than a battery creature led to an abattoir without ever having known the open fields of Jerez and beyond where the modern fighting bull is bred in conditions which would generate the admiration of any animal lover.

It is impossible to offer a judgment on this topic in a few words, even if one knew what judgment to give, so I shall say little more. The season in Andalucia is generally from April to September, with *corridas* on most Sundays. Hotel reception desks are a sound source of advice on how to get hold of tickets – which are expensive – and you are likely to see top rank matadors in the three best rings on this itinerary at Seville, Ronda and El Puerto de Santa María.

One should not be fooled into thinking that the *corrida* is all seriousness. Occasionally fights are interrupted by *el espontáneo*, the spontaneous amateur matador who leaps out of the crowd and into the ring to tackle the bull before the professional has had a chance. Several well-known matadors have started their careers in this way, though the action inevitably leads to a limited banishment from *corridas* throughout the country.

In the likeable little bar of El Portón, in the street of General Polavieja off the Plaza Nueva, you will find a photograph of one of Seville's *espontáneos*, as well as several excellent tapas and breakfast *tortas*. The gentleman concerned clearly survived the bout, in 1959, since his own writing on the picture dedicated it to his friends. The photograph shows a portly Sevilliano, in suit and broad hat, facing up to a bemused looking bull and looking every day of 70... which was, indeed, his age. A delighted crowd applauds him in the background.

Overnight in Seville.

ACCOMMODATION

See page pp. 36-9 for hotels in Seville.

EATING OUT

Burladero
Canalejas 1
Seville
Tel: 222900

Dedicated lovers of the bullring have always adored the Burladero, Hemingway among them. Items from the *corrida* decorate the walls in this serious, quiet restaurant which makes few concessions to new fashions in Spanish cooking. Fillets of sole with langoustine in champagne, beef fillets with green pepper sauce for two, and 'English roast beef' are regulars, but there is always a daily special. The wine list covers Spanish reds, particularly fine Riojas, comprehensively. The Burladero is a Sevillian institution and, like most institutions, has its critics on occasions. However, the food is normally excellent and the atmosphere inimitable.

Open every day
Credit cards: American Express, Diner's Club, Eurocard, Visa
Rating ****

Oriza
San Fernando 41
Seville
Tel: 227211

Modern Spanish cuisine, featuring light salads, saffron sauces, and imaginative fish dishes, in a pleasant first floor dining room close to the María Luisa park. The bar below serves fine tapas but is usually crowded by 9pm.

Oriza contd
Ajo blanco, mousse of sea bass, confit of duck, and salmon dishes feature regularly on a menu which is a paragon of modern Spanish cuisine.

Closed Sundays and August
Credit cards: American Express, Diner's Club, Eurocard, Visa
Rating ****

Figon del Cabildo
Pl del Cabildo
Seville
Tel: 220117

A blend of modern and traditional Spanish cuisine close to the Cathedral. Creamed asparagus with langoustines, salad of eels and endives, scrambled eggs with wild mushrooms, and a wide range of fish and seafood dishes.

Closed Sundays
Credit cards: American Express, Diner's Club, Eurocard, Visa
Rating ****

La Isla
Arfe 25
Seville
Tel: 215376

Sound paella, Basque fish dishes and roast lamb only a few yards from the Figon del Cabildo.

Closed August
Credit cards: American Express, Diner's Club, Eurocard, Visa
Rating ****

La Judería
Cano y Cueto 13
Seville
Tel: 412052

One of the best bets close to the Barrio de Santa Cruz, the Judería serves predictable, but well cooked, traditional Spanish food in a spacious dining room. First rate gazpacho, sucking lamb, sea bass, and changing specials of the day.

Closed Tuesdays
Credit cards: American Express, Diner's Club, Eurocard, Visa
Rating ***

For a guide to eating tapas, see pp, 56-8.

Holy Week celebrations, Seville

DAY 3

On foot to the richly stocked art gallery, the Museo de Bellas Artes, which has the finest collection of works of the Sevillian school in the world, the Casa de Pilatos, an old mansion decorated in Moslem, Roman and Renaissance styles with fine gardens, and then to the former local quarter of the Barrio de Santa Cruz, with its picturesque alleys and small squares.

Overnight in Seville.

Map reference
Seville   37° 25´N 5° 58´W

Seville

Breakfast in Seville.

Museo de Bellas Artes

As befits a city of its stature, Seville has a great art gallery, and one housed in such splendid surroundings that it will impress even the few who find its paintings uninteresting. The Museo de Bellas Artes also makes a convenient starting point for a walking tour of the one remaining unseen part of central Seville.

The gallery can be found in the northern part of the city, housed in a former monastery. It is within walking distance of the Plaza Nueva, but if your hotel is more distant it may be easier to take a taxi there and continue the rest of the way on foot. Substantial renovations during 1988 mean that it is impossible, at the time of writing, to give a precise description of the way the gallery will be ordered when later visitors arrive. The contents are unlikely to change, however, and it is these, and their surroundings, which are the principal attractions.

As one would expect, the bulk of the exhibition is devoted to the finer works of the Sevillian School which was very much a part of the decadent, affluent city of the 17th century. The school produced work which was both religious and, at the same time, worldly, only occasionally drifting into florid romanticism of the kind typified by the cherubs in Murillo's Vision of Saint Anthony of Padua seen in the Cathedral, the picture in which, one may recall, a tasteful thief removed the saint's worthwhile head and left the rest behind.

Murillo is the most famous member of the Sevillian school, a prolific artist rarely known to turn down a commission, even when inspiration was later seen to be lacking. The museum has a rich collection of Murillo's work from all stages of his career. Several are versions of the Immaculate Conception, a subject on which he was forever called to canvas by commissioning clergy. A room is also dedicated to the work of Valdés Leal, now less well known though, in his time, an artist who was thought to be virtually Murillo's equal. It was his nightmares on the wall of the Hospital de la Caridad, but the museum's collection shows that the artist also had a more conventional repertoire, stretching beyond the general range of religious subjects which kept a painter alive in those days.

The third famous figure was Zurbarán, well represented here in a superb series of paintings of Sevillian women in religious dress, as well as in a canvas which wins more technical acclaim, The Apotheosis of St Thomas Aquinas. A self portrait by El Greco, works by Velasquez and a collection of more modern Spanish paintings complete the inventory of a gallery which must be counted one of the most enjoyable in Spain, as much for its surroundings and atmosphere as the art it contains.

From the museum, one should walk to the Plaza Nueva, the central square which is a focal point of everyday Sevillian life. It is here that many of the more important parades of Holy Week gather, close to the steps of the old council building, the Ayuntamiento, which stands at the centre of the square. The Plaza is a busy commercial centre for banks, both foreign and domestic, and the old street of Sierpes, which leads from it to the north, is one of the most active shopping areas of the city. The 16th-century Ayuntamiento is a classical building, odd in that it is substantially decorated on one side only, that facing away from the Plaza. The delicate stonework represents the best of Plateresque, the ornate style dating from the 16th century so named because it resembles the work of silversmiths.

Leaving the square by the corner after Sierpes, you soon reach the Church of El Salvador, an enormous hulk of religious masonry under restoration. It is not the most memorable of churches, but the streets behind it are unusual. Córdoba, directly behind the church, is shaded during the height of summer by large blinds hung across the street in the manner of a middle Eastern souk. San Isidoro leads to the church of the same name, and a more agreeable one it is than El Salvador. Beyond it, the street of Aguilas leads to the Casa de Pilatos, Pilate's House, one of the city's most sumptuous private residences and one which earns its keep by accepting visitors.

This part of the city is perpetually undergoing restoration work and street signs – and sometimes names – may be unreliable. Asking for the Casa de Pilatos, or the well-known Calle de Aguilas, will set the visitor bemused by the labyrinth of narrow alleys back on the right track.

The Casa de Pilatos

The Casa de Pilatos is so named because it was believed, probably erroneously, that the mansion was based upon the original plan of the house of Pontius Pilate in Jerusalem. This tale naturally became accepted as fact in Seville, and the house itself at one time played an integral part in the Holy Week ceremonies, like some Spanish station of the cross. Its interest for the visitor is less apocryphal; the house is a well preserved example of both *mudéjar* and Renaissance styles – for the technically minded – and a picturesque, upper class mansion, with fine halls and gardens – for the everyday sightseer.

It was built in the 16th century, on two storeys which enables the present owner to charge twice for the privilege of seeing it all, once per floor. The second storey is by no means as essential as the first and may be omitted by the budget conscious, halving the price but reducing the enjoyment by no more than a fifth.

After being relieved of one's pesetas, the way is shown into a courtyard in which Roman, Moslem and Christian influences mingle with only the occasional aesthetic protests on the sidelines. Four Roman statues dominate the patio and around the walls there are busts of famous Roman emperors with a head of Charles V thrown in for extra measure (it clearly paid to keep good relations with the reigning monarchy, and what better way than to compare him with Augustus and Caesar?). On one side lies the Salon del Pretorio, a handsome chamber leading to a small garden. There are halls of a similar, if less impressive, nature around the patio, and a sumptuous garden maintained with a care beyond the reach of the average municipal horticulturist (those of Granada's Generalife being a rare exception).

To visit the first floor, you must wait for someone to open the door, and then a close watch is maintained, for part is still used as private rooms and some of the 18th- and 19th-century furniture is valuable. The paintings are mainly copies, but one can get a good impression of how the upper class Spanish family would like to live, and for 200 pesetas that may be a fair return if no bargain.

Barrio de Santa Cruz

To the south of the mansion, reached by any number of alleys, lies the Barrio de Santa Cruz. I have left this, the best known of the tourist haunts of Seville, to the last precisely because I would not like the visitor to come to believe that the Barrio is the focal point of Seville. It is a charming neighbourhood of small streets, where flowers tumble over iron grills and singers and guitarists gather in pretty little squares trying to earn the odd peseta. To the south it leads into the colourful Murillo Gardens which adjoin those of the Alcázar and are a pleasant spot to rest after a hard day's walking. There is only one 'sight' and that is the 17th-century Hospital de Venerable Sacerdotes, which has several good canvases and a characterful, if crumbling, interior. But I would not regard it as essential, and the visiting arrangements – you must call for the attendant – are unreliable.

The trouble with the Barrio is that, unlike the similar Judería in Córdoba, it has now wholeheartedly abandoned itself to the pursuit of the tourist peseta. Few Sevillianos would eat in any of the restaurants, not even, sadly, the ancient hostel Laurel close by the Hospital. In the evening, only parties of puzzled tourists wander the streets, baffled that this rather quiet and artificial corner of the city seems to be the centre of famous, vivid Seville.

A taxi to Triana, or even a walk by the Guadalquivir, would reveal what the locals really do at night. This is not to say that the Barrio is unenjoyable; simply that it should not be regarded as the natural haunt of the visitor, for if it is then you will come away with a wholly inaccurate picture of life in this most colourful of cities.

Overnight in Seville.

ACCOMMODATION

See pp. 36-9 for hotels.

EATING OUT – Tapas

The tapas bars of Seville are so plentiful and wide-ranging in style that it is sometimes a wonder that anyone eats in the city's restaurants at all. An evening spent sampling tapas should be a casual one, with no set route or menu in mind, for much of the pleasure of this very Spanish way of eating comes from the discovery of some new delicacy in a little neighbourhood *bodega*. There will be disappointments, of course. Once, in the middle of a fair in Seville, a *bodega* owner implored me to try his new speciality *delicias de la casa*; they turned out to be merely crabsticks. But tapas are so cheap and so small that the odd disaster hardly matters, and there is always something around the corner to dispel any dubious or disappointing tastes.

It would be fatal to outline a particular tapas route through the city. Bars and standards change quickly, so you must use your own initiative. But I will offer a few starting points and tips, and some encouragement to cross the river into Triana, the true flamenco neighbourhood of Seville, full of fine food, local music, little ceramics factories producing handmade tiles and pottery, and more atmosphere per square inch than you will find in a mile of the Barrio de Santa Cruz.

Tapas, which are often called *aperitivos* in Seville, are tiny portions of food served over the counter of a bar or *bodega*. They may be a few shrimps, a handful of peppers fried in oil with garlic, or a local kebab, the *pinchito*, flavoured with herbs. The cost is *usually* very low, but you should be warned that there are a few tapas which can be expensive. These include all large prawns and shellfish and wind-cured mountain ham, *jamón serrano*. Most tapas bars have a small card listing what they have to offer with prices. Others chalk the daily list on a board. A few simply tell the customer what is on offer, and in Triana a couple of bars have turned this into a little ritual in which the barman will, at the speed of light, rattle off a string of names until the customer stops at one he likes. The staff of the Bar Noly, in Pagés del Corro, Triana, can recite a catalogue of more than 70 different tapas in this fashion.

A comprehensive guide to the tapas of Spain would require a volume the size of the average dictionary. Every region has its specialities, and every city has bars which specialise in the tapas of other regions. So, if you walk down the street of Harinas, just behind the Hotel Inglaterra, you will find the Rincón del Gallo, specialising in Galician food. The woman cook ladles whole octopus into a pan, there is the Galician *empanada*, a thin savoury pie, and *ribeiro*, the young, cidery white wine of the province drunk from shallow pot cups. Ordinary back streets contain many such little discoveries. In the central city, the area behind the Plaza Nueva is one of the most fruitful for tapas hunting. Close to the Rincón del Gallo is Seville-Jabugo (Castelar 1), serving some of the best mountain ham, sausage, cheese and *cocido* – chick pea and sausage stew – in the city.

Bear in mind that many of the best restaurants also have bars which serve tapas from the same kitchen. This offers an excellent way of weighing up a restaurant without sitting down to eat a full meal. Of the two expensive restaurants mentioned in the previous day's section, both Burladero and Oriza have excellent bars which serve reasonably priced and interesting tapas, such as a whole quail in almond sauce at the Burladero's La Tasca bar and langoustine stuffed with caviar at the Oriza.

Triana is only a short walk away across the bridge at the end of Reyes Católicos. This leads directly into the Plaza del Altozano and the main street of the neighbourhood, San Jacinto. There is a wealth of tapas bars, many specialising in seafood, *langostinos* from Sanlúcar, legs of spider crab (*patas rusas*), and many different kinds of prawns including the tiny *camárones*, eaten whole. Minute omelettes of shrimp (*tortillitas de camarones*), fishcakes of salt cod (*buñuelos de bacalao*), cod's roe with tomatoes, onions and peppers (*huevos aliñadas*), fried mixed fish (*pescaíto frito*), and mussels (*mejillones*) are common dishes. There is such competition here that you are unlikely to fare badly. The expensive restaurant of Sevilla-Sanlúcar Mar, at the end of the bridge, has a tapas bar, and close by you will find excellent food at the Bar Los Dos Hermanos and Bar Emilio, a little further along San Jacinto.

Small *bodegas* line the street of Betis, running along this bank of the Guadalquivir, catering for the evening riverside walkers. The street of Pagés del Corro, which runs from San Jacinto to the Plaza de Cuba, has several promising tapas bars, and in Antillano Campos, a narrow road parallel with San Jacinto, there are a number of atmospheric little *bodegas*, one of the best being Bar Las Golodrinas, which is run by a former mayor of Triana. Here you will find superb olives, laced with herbs and lemon, salads of carrot (*zanahoria*), pepper (*pimiento*), and beetroot (*remolacha*), tiny steak (*punto de solomillo*) and mushrooms grilled with oil, garlic and herbs (*champiñón a la plancha*).

Black pudding and blood sausage (*morcilla* and *sangre encebollada*) are two of the many popular spiced sausages, while *pringá* is a tasty speciality composed of the morsels of different sausages and hams, fried and served in a small bun, like a tiny hamburger. *Guisas caseros* are home-made stews, *brocheta de solomillo* a steak kebab, and *cazuelas* casseroles, often flavoured with sherry. Everywhere one can see those standbys of the modern Spanish kitchen, sardines (*sardinas*), kidneys in sherry (*riñones al Jerez*), squid (*calamares*), cockles (*berberechos*), and small clams (*almejas*).

For the linguistically unsure a simple '*que es...*' will usually ensure that the barman will point to the speciality in question among the dishes behind the counter. Even for the Spanish, verbal descriptions of local tapas tend to be restricted to *carne* (meat), *pescado* (fish), or *marisco* (shellfish). Tapas hunting is both a challenge and an adventure, and one pretty soon begins to get the hang of the game. The Spanish are welcoming to foreigners who make the attempt to get to know something of the real Spain, particularly in Triana which is a working class neighbourhood usually ignored by tourists. A few words of Spanish and an interest in the different dishes on offer will usually unlock a *bodega* proprietor's tongue in an instant.

For restaurants, see pp. 47-9.

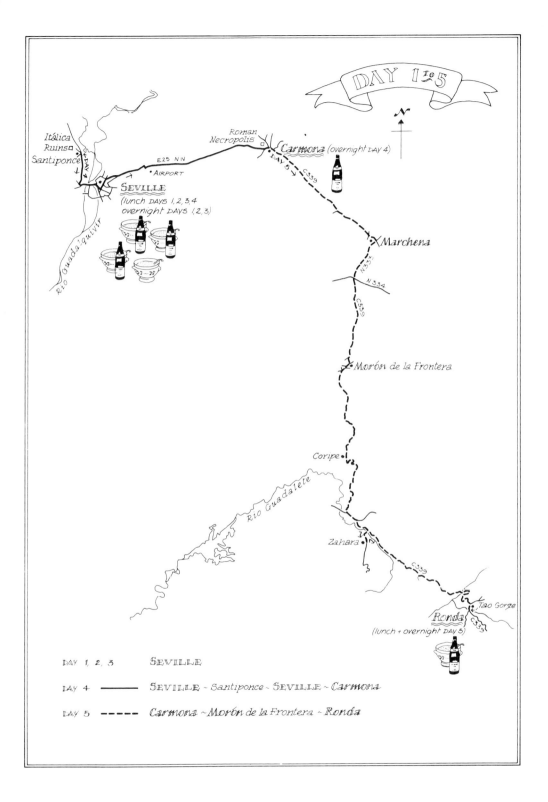

DAY 1 to 5

N

Itálica
Ruins
Santiponce

E25 NN

Roman
Necropolis

Carmona (overnight DAY 4)

Airport

DAY 4

SEVILLE
(lunch DAYS 1, 2, 3, 4
overnight DAYS 1, 2, 3)

DAY 5

C339

Rio Guadalquivir

Marchena

N 333

N 334

C339

Morón de la Frontera

Coripe

Rio Guadalete

Zahara

C339

Ronda
(lunch + overnight DAY 5)

Tao Gorge

C339

DAY 1, 2, 3   SEVILLE

DAY 4 —————— SEVILLE ~ Santiponce ~ SEVILLE ~ Carmona

DAY 5 - - - - - Carmona ~ Morón de la Frontera ~ Ronda

Torre del Oro, Seville

DAY 4

Seville to Carmona via the Roman ruins of Italica, about 40 miles.

A brief excursion north of the city leads to the extensive ruins of the former Roman city of Italica, with its well preserved amphitheatre, now scene of summer arts events. The modern town of Santiponce nearby houses the monastery of San Isidoro del Campo where the Spanish hero Guzmán El Bueno is buried. Returning to Seville for lunch, the route continues along the busy road to Madrid as far as Carmona, a small town with a famous Roman necropolis, a picturesque old quarter, and a parador housed in a former Arab fortress.

Overnight in Carmona.

Route shown p. 59.

Map references
Seville	37°25′N 5°58′W
Santiponce	37°27′N 6°02′W
Carmona	37°29′N 5°38′W

Seville

Breakfast in Seville.

The capital of Roman Spain was Córdoba, but there were important settlements throughout Andalucia, one of the largest being three miles north of Seville. Italica, like all cities of the Roman empire, was no colonial outpost, but a functioning arm of Rome itself. A number of famous Romans were born in Spain, the emperor Hadrian in Italica itself.

Santiponce

The ruins lie off the N630 which is signposted to another former Roman settlement, Mérida in Extremadura, just before the Huelva motorway. At the modern town of Santiponce, there is a substantial and impressive amphitheatre which is used for modern dance and theatrical events during the summer. Italica was created for soldiers involved in the second Punic War against the Carthaginians, a campaign fought across the breadth of the Iberian peninsula and beyond. The main Roman settlement, with its mosaics and rather shapeless ruins, is a little distance away, shrugging off the siesta to stay open until 5.30pm weekdays, and 3pm on Sundays.

Santiponce also houses the monastery of San Isidoro del Campo where you will find the tomb of one of Spain's great heroes, Guzmán El Bueno, buried with his wife and son in the monastery he founded in 1298, almost two centuries before Moslem rule was finally curtailed in Granada less than 200 miles away. The story of Guzmán is best told later, at the scene of the stoic heroism which is the source of his fame. Suffice to say here that Guzmán is a figure as charismatic in Spain as the Black Prince is in England, and of particular interest to anyone taking this itinerary through western Andalucia. The route covers the site of the victory where, at the cost of a son, he won his reputation and also the small white mountain town where he was killed in a border skirmish. The effigies of the victor and his wife are the work of Montañes and must, accordingly, be treated as works of art rather than record; more than 300 years separate Guzmán's death from their creation.

This brief excursion can be completed easily in the space of a morning, returning to Seville for lunch and then leaving by the main road to Madrid, signposted at various times for the capital, for Córdoba, and, on one occasion, even for Carmona itself. The NIV from here runs in a busy throng of traffic past the airport of Seville and across the broad, flat plain of the Guadalquivir, the hottest region of Spain where temperatures may rise to 100°F (38°C) and beyond at the height of summer. Ecija, the first main town beyond Carmona, is known as 'the frying pan of Spain', for reasons which are obvious to any midsummer visitor.

Carmona

Carmona rises ahead from the traffic dust, with the usual raggle taggle collection of small industrial buildings that precede the ancient settlements of Spain. Only when you have passed this unremarkable suburb does the promise of Carmona become apparent. A historic city gate – part Roman, part Arab, part Christian – appears at a set of busy traffic lights, and through it the cobbled street which leads into the heart of the old town, encircled by battlements and protected by three castles.

Follow the signs for the parador, since it is the only worthwhile place to stay and eat, and the state hotel is housed in one of the three Arab fortresses of Carmona. A winding route through narrow alleys finally leads to the Alcázar del Rey Don Pedro, without doubt one of the best of the converted fortresses which make up the pearls of the parador chain. From its walls, one can survey the flat Guadalquivir plain for miles around. Pedro the Cruel, the 14th-century creator of Seville's Alcázar, was a frequent visitor and made the castle as ornate as his principal residence. It was from here that the infamous monarch departed for his final battle, at Montiel, where he was killed by his stepbrother. Little survives from those times, and for many years the Alcázar was derelict until the promise of visitors' pesetas brought about its resurrection as a delightful parador.

Carmona is a town that likes to flaunt its history. Visitors will be told that it can claim the oldest continuous population in Europe, since it has been settled for more than 5,000 years, that the Puerta de Sevilla, the ancient gate by which one enters the old town, forms part of the most complicated defensive enclosure in Spain, and that the turret of Pedro's now busy Alcázar is the oldest artillery emplacement in Europe. There is a touch of truth to many of these claims; Carmona has been inhabited since the earliest days of man, and one need only walk the streets of the old town to understand the historical importance of the community. The mansions speak of wealth and power, the religious buildings of San Blas, Santa María, and Santiago and Santa Clara contain Roman, Visigothic, Moslem and Renaissance elements.

The Roman necropolis lies beyond the old town, off the road to Seville. There is a profusion of circular family graves, and you can descend into some to see the stone caskets of different generations within the hollowed-out walls. The so-called Elephant Tomb, a series of chambers, one of which contains a statue of the animal, is thought to be a ceremonial section of the necropolis where mourners partook of a banquet after the cremation ceremony. Dining rooms, a kitchen and water channels are pointed out to visitors as proof that the chambers were designed for use by the living and not the dead.

The largest tomb is that of Servilia, a Roman noblewoman who died in the 1st century AD while visiting Spain. Unusually, the body was interred not, as was the local custom, cremated, probably to suit the taste of her Roman relatives. The tomb is essentially a recreation of a large Roman villa of the time. Many of the more valuable items found during excavation work have been moved elsewhere, principally to the archeological museum in Seville. But the small museum attached to the site has an interesting and well-displayed collection of smaller items, notably lamps and small pottery, and the remains of a ribald fresco which seems a little out of place in a burial ground.

The old town can be seen in a few hours from the parador. Turning right at the exit takes the walker past the Church of Santiago to the Puerta de Córdoba, the eastern door of the walled town. Then follow the northern boundary, past the Convent of Santa Clara and the Prioral of Santa María into the main square, now named after the liberator of Seville, Ferdinand the Saint. The church of San Pedro, which lies outside the city walls, opposite the Puerta de Sevilla, is highly ornate baroque and rather swamped by the heavy traffic (Carmona is in desperate need of a bypass). The necropolis apart, the town's interest lies behind the walls and the gates of Seville and Córdoba.

Overnight in Carmona.

ACCOMMODATION

Parador Nacional Alcázar del Rey Don Pedro
Carmona
Tel: 141010/140160

Splendid historical parador with views over the Guadalquivir plain. This is the only hotel in Carmona and advance bookings are advisable. If you are unable to book a room, it would be best to stay an extra night in Seville and visit Carmona during the day. The parador has an attractive arched restaurant serving local dishes and standard Andalucian cuisine: *ajo blanco* and *corderito*, leg of baby lamb, are typical dishes. There are no other restaurants of note in Carmona, but a profusion of small bars serving the usual range of tapas. In spite of its past, modern Carmona is not a town of sophistication, so I suggest the parador as the best base for both accommodation and eating.

Open all year
Rooms: 59
Credit cards: American Express, Diner's Club, Eurocard, Visa
Rating ****

CARMONA: USEFUL INFORMATION	
Tourist office:	there is no official office but the parador carries tourist information
Population:	22,779

Carmona

DAY 5

Carmona to Ronda via Morón de la Frontera and Zahara, about 75 miles.

The route turns south from the Guadalquivir plain and enters the mountains which lead to the remote town of Ronda, in a dramatic setting overlooking a rocky gorge. Two picturesque rural towns, Morón and Zahara, the latter set on a hill overlooking the valley of the Guadalete river, are passed en route.

Overnight in Ronda.

Route shown p. 59.

Map references

Carmona	37° 29´N 5° 38´W
Morón de la Frontera	37° 08´N 5° 28´W
Zahara	36° 50´N 5° 25´W
Ronda	36° 45´N 5° 10´W

Breakfast in Carmona.

A reasonably early start from Carmona will bring the visitor to Ronda in good time for lunch. The roads are not of the best, but the countryside is a pleasant change from the flatness of the Seville plain, rising into the heights of the mountains which have protected Ronda from the outside world.

Leaving Carmona by the Puerta de Córdoba, a right turn marked to Marchena appears a few yards along the main road to Madrid. This joins the N333 as far as the N334 main Seville-Granada highway where a minor road is marked for Morón de la Frontera. At Morón there is a ruined castle and an old quarter full of the character of rural Spain. From here until the route reaches the N340 at the Mediterranean coast the bustle and clamour of the modern world will, to a great extent, be left behind.

Zahara

The C339, signposted for Coripe, leaves Morón and rises into the northernmost mountains of the range that dominates the southern corner of Andalucia, a region of small, remote towns which have little contact with the tourist invasion of the coast and the big cities. The route turns left, briefly, along the main Arcos-Antequera road, then branches right, signposted for Ronda. Zahara is set back from the road, a photogenic town surmounting a hill overlooking the valley of the Guadalete, now being turned into a new dam. Visitors rarely reach Zahara, yet it is a charming place, with relics of old walls from Moslem times and views of the unspoilt mountains which surround it. Little has changed in Zahara in the last two decades, save the general improvement in living standards which can be seen throughout Spain.

Ronda

This is the most scenic approach to Ronda. The town appears on the horizon out of nowhere, its mansions lining the edge of the gorge which has made it famous. This dramatic mountain setting has attracted visitors for more than a century. To the upper class members of the British establishment of Gibraltar of old, the town represented a pleasant escape from the

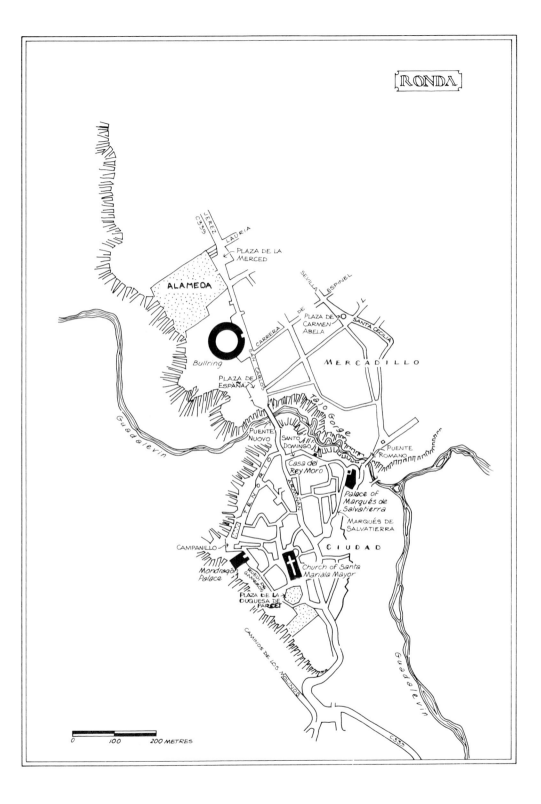

RONDA

JEREZ C 339
LAURIA
PLAZA DE LA MERCED

ALAMEDA

SEVILLA ESPINEL
PLAZA DE CARMEN-ABELA
SANTA CECILIA

DE
CARRERA
SAN CARLOS
Bullring

MERCADILLO

PLAZA DE ESPAÑA

Tajo Gorge

Guadalevin

PUENTE NUOVO

SANTO DOMINGO

PUENTE ROMANO

Casa del Rey Moro

Palace of Marqués de Salvatierra

MARQUÉS DE SALVATIERRA

TENORIO
ARMIÑAN

CAMPANILLO

CIUDAD

Mondragón Palace

CUESTA DE GAMEGOS

Church of Santa Mariala Mayor

PLAZA DE LA DUQUESA DE PARSET

CAMINOS DE LOS MOLINOS

Guadalevin

C 339

0   100   200 METRES

Rock's boiling summers. And to the modern tourist on the Costa del Sol, it is packaged as a glimpse of real Spain away from the tourist resorts.

Ronda has proved a continual source of discomfiture for those who have tried to tame it. Its inhabitants have mounted determined rearguard campaigns again invaders, both Moslem and Christian, using the town's natural geographic advantages to the full. The remote sierra, and its back routes to the duty free port of Gibraltar, have encouraged smuggling well into this century, and more than a few Ronda families can tell tales of the contraband activities of close relatives.

Lunch in Ronda.

The town has a spectacular location, divided as it is by the enormous gorge or *tajo* which was often its last line of defence against attackers. To the south lies the early Arab settlement now known as the Ciudad, an area of palatial mansions and picturesque streets. Across the gorge, spanned by Puente Nuevo, lies the newer quarter of Mercadillo, now the principal residential and shopping area. Ronda is a compact town, quite easily seen in one day. It copes with the daytime tourist coaches from the Costa del Sol with little enthusiasm; the 'natural reticence' of the mountain community looks very like dourness in another guise.

A tour of the town should begin at the Alameda, the park which overlooks the gorge from Mercadillo, a few hundred yards down the street from the Hotel Reina Victoria. The view is virtually identical to that seen from the garden of the town's most expensive hotel. The edge of the attractive park hangs over the beetling rocks of the ravine in a fashion which may deter the faint-hearted. The surrounding mountains of the Sierra Rondeña, stony and largely bare, stretch to the horizon. The one disappointment may be the rather puny stream which runs through the foot of the gorge; it was not always so. A dam scheme has reduced the flow of what was once a river to today's trickle.

Walking towards the Puente Nuevo, you will reach the bullring which, within Spain, is the town's principal claim to fame. It was here, in this remote mountain location, that an innovation was introduced into bullfighting which – no doubt to the anger of modern animal lovers – probably saved the custom from extinction. Until the 18th century, bulls were fought from horseback, as they still are in a few locations in Spain today. The sport fell out of favour in this fashion, and was only revived when a formidable Ronda character called Pedro Romero came up with a new variation on the bullfighting theme: fighting on foot.

The *corrida* once again became fashionable, and the rules established by Romero in the ring at Ronda are now current throughout Spain. For the aficionado, a visit to the *corrida* here is an essential act of homage, and that American follower of the matadors, Hemingway, was a regular visitor to the Ronda ring.

Whatever one thinks of bullfighting, the ring is undeniably an attractive building, classically proportioned with two storeys. Visitors can wander around it for a small entrance fee during the day, and see a small museum containing bullfighting memorabilia. A brief glance at some of the blood-stained tunics shows that some of Romero's followers did not have the luck of their esteemed predecessor, who died in his bed, having killed his last bull at the age of 80. Romero is remembered each September at a bull-fighting festival in which the participants wear flamboyant historic costumes based on those seen in paintings of *corridas* by Goya.

From the ring, it is a short walk to the Plaza de España, the rather chaotic little square which stands in front of the Puente Nuevo on the Mercadillo side. Here may be found the tourist information office, an essential stop for anyone wishing to visit one of the palaces in the Ciudad, since virtually all, at the time of writing, are in private hands, and throw open their doors irregularly if at all. The bridge itself deserves attention, being built from foundations which begin 400 feet below on the river bed, so sheer are the sides of the *tajo*. The creator of this extraordinary piece of architecture never lived to see its completion, falling to his death from its heights shortly before the bridge was finished.

There are satisfying views from both sides: of the gorge and the two smaller bridges, one Arabic, the other Roman, to the left, and, in the opposite direction, of the grand mansions of the Ciudad itself, clinging to the cliff edge to give their inhabitants the best of the town's extraordinary views.

On reaching the old Arab town, bear right, along Tenorio, ignoring the signs which try to tempt one downhill to the old quarter on the opposite side of the road. You will pass row upon row of typical Ronda mansions: high-roomed and grand, with ornate studded doors on the street, and large, panoramic rooms at the rear overlooking the *tajo*. A small park, the Campanillo, opens onto the gorge, and one can look back to the Alameda in Mercadillo and down to the remains of old Arab mills in the river bed.

Leaving by the narrow alley at the end of the Plaza, one reaches the Mondragon Palace, one of a number of Arab palaces restored for later Christian use. A few hundred yards further lies the Church of Santa María la Mayor, built on the site of Ronda's main mosque. There is now a pleasant square in front of the church, the Plaza de la Duquesa de Parcet. The church authorities have seen fit to charge a small entrance fee, though there is little to see inside the building except for one, non-Christian curiosity. This is the original mihrab of the old mosque, the most holy place of worship for the followers of Islam, uncovered close to the ticket desk and largely passed over by the casual visitor. The Arabic script and ornate stucco have a familiar look to anyone who has wandered around Seville, and show distinctly better taste than the baroque Christian interior.

On leaving the church, walk a little distance back towards Mercadillo on the busy main road, then branch right at the small lane which begins with an unmistakable minaret now built into a private house.

The street leads directly down to the last two famous buildings of the Ciudad. The first is the Palace of the Marques de Salvatierra, distinguished by a set of finely carved grotesque figures depicting savages from the New World, a subject seen elsewhere in Andalucia in buildings of this time. A little way up the hill stands the green-roofed Casa del Rey Moro, House of the Moorish King, an Arabic palace currently in private hands and closed to the public. This, according to tradition, was the palace of the Moslem ruler, and many local tales abound of the foul deeds supposedly carried out within its walls. One tale is with foundation, however; there really is a tunnel which runs all the way from the palace gardens down to the river bed, a feature which doubtless proved useful in times of siege.

Continuing down the hill, one reaches the Arabic bridge across the gorge. To the right is the smaller Roman bridge, and close to it the remains of Arab baths. On the other side, we have yet another varied view of the houses and walls of the Ciudad. The steep hill of Santa Cecilia brings us back into the heart of Mercadillo.

Overnight in Ronda.

ACCOMMODATION

Reina Victoria
Dr Fleming, 25
Ronda
Tel: 871240

Ronda's most fashionable place to stay, with well-kept and extensive gardens overlooking the gorge. It was to here that the poet Rilke came when suffering from tuberculosis. His room is preserved and there is a statue in his memory in the gardens. The situation and views are perfect; the hotel itself looks a little tired at times, and service could be better. It is not yet priced as a luxury hotel, however, and represents good value and Ronda's only genuinely memorable hotel.

Open all year
Rooms: 88
Facilities: gardens, outdoor pool
Credit cards: American Express, Diner's Club, Eurocard, Visa
Rating ****

El Tajo
Cruz Verde 7
Ronda
Tel: 876236

Quiet and inexpensive hotel, principally for Spanish business visitors, in the centre of Mercadillo. The rooms are comfortable and there is a lock-up garage next to the hotel. Can be difficult to find for the first-time visitor; look for signposts close to the bullring.

Open all year
Rooms: 37
Credit cards: American Express, Visa
Rating **

EATING OUT

Don Miguel
Pl de España 3
Ronda
Tel: 871090

In spite of its setting at the heart of tourist Ronda, the Don Miguel maintains high standards, and the tables, set on terraces on the side of the *tajo*, have memorable views. Mountain ham, *plato rondeña*, which includes fried eggs, local sausage and *migas*, and hare are among the meat specialities. Fresh fish is imported daily from the Atlantic for dishes such as sole in champagne.

Closed Sundays and late January to mid-February
Credit cards: American Express, Diner's Club, Eurocard, Visa
Rating ***

Pedro Romero
Virgen de la Paz 18
Ronda
Tel: 871061

Game and meat dishes feature heavily on a fairly standard menu designed to catch the eye of visitors to the nearby bullring.

Open every day
Credit cards: American Express, Diner's Club, Eurocard, Visa
Rating ***

RONDA: USEFUL INFORMATION	
Tourist office:	Plaza de España 1
	Tel: 871272
Population:	31,383
Altitude:	2,450 feet

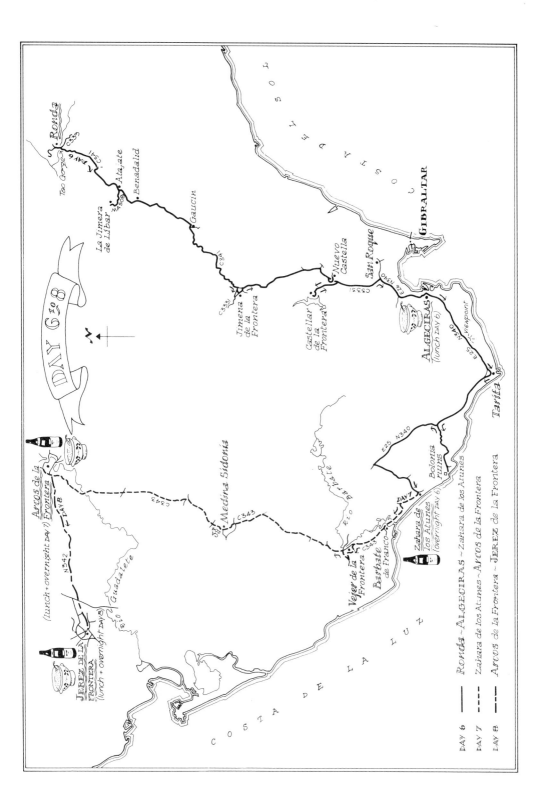

DAY 6 to 8

Ronda

To Gorge
C-335
C-341
PAY 6
Atajate
Benadalid
MA-509
La Jimera
de Líbar
Gaucin
C-341
C-333
Jimera
de la
Frontera

Medina Sidonia
C-343
C-343

Arcos de la
Frontera
(lunch + overnight day 7)
PAY 8

JEREZ DE LA
FRONTERA
(lunch + overnight day 8)
N-342
Guadalete

N-542

Vejer de la
Frontera
Barbate
de Franco
Zahara de
los Atunes
(overnight day 6)
DAY 7
C-343

Castellar
de la
Frontera
C-331
Nuevo
Castella
MA-500
San Roque
E-15 N-340
N-340
ALGECIRAS
(lunch Day 6)
viewpoint

GIBRALTAR

COSTA DEL SOL

E-25 N-340
Bolonia
ruins
Tarifa

COSTA DE LA LUZ

DAY 6 ———— Ronda ~ ALGECIRAS ~ Zahara de los Atunes
DAY 7 --------- Zahara de los Atunes ~ Arcos de la Frontera
DAY 8 – – – – Arcos de la Frontera ~ JEREZ de la Frontera

Puente Nuevo, Ronda

DAY 6

Ronda to Zahara de los Atunes, about 110 miles.

The route travels south, through the mountains of the Sierra Rondeña, to the Mediterranean coast, and then rounds Gibraltar, reaching the Atlantic at Spain's southernmost point, Tarifa. This is the beginning of the Costa de la Luz, a largely unspoilt coast; the day ends at Zahara de los Atunes, a small tunny fishing village.

Overnight in Zahara de los Atunes.

Route shown p. 75.

Map references

Ronda	36° 45´N 5° 10´W
Atajate	36° 38´N 5° 15´W
Benadalid	36° 35´N 5° 17´W
Jimena de la Frontera	36° 28´N 5° 25´W
Castellar de la Frontera	36° 20´N 5° 25´W
Algeciras	36° 10´N 5° 28´W
Tarifa	36° 01´N 5° 36´W
Zahara de los Atunes	36° 09´N 5° 51´W

Breakfast in Ronda.

The mountain area running west of Ronda is known as the Frontera, the frontier which was once the continuous battleground between Moslem and Christian forces. Many towns still bear the suffix *de la Frontera*, the best known being Jerez. The communities of the mountains are often collectively known as the *pueblos blancos*, the white towns. The reason soon becomes obvious, when observing the ragged lines of white houses scattered across the bare peaks, betraying their North African origins in narrow streets and the Moorish grills which cover the windows of old houses, an adaptation of an old Moslem device designed to allow the occupant to see into the street without being seen from outside.

It is a part of Spain rarely visited by the foreign tourist, and one which can detain the traveller for several days, wandering from pueblo to pueblo in the sierra bounded by Arcos de la Frontera, the bay of Algeciras and Ronda. Here there is time for only one excursion through the pueblos blancos, but it is one of the best, travelling through the lower part of the range past several archetypal small towns.

Leave Ronda by the Ciudad, over the Puente Nuevo and follows the signs for Algeciras, driving quickly into the open sierra. Mule tracks still cross the barren land, and one can appreciate how difficult the authorities must have found policing the contraband run through these peaks from Gibraltar. Smuggling bands were common until the 1930s, and this was one of their favourite routes. The small town of Atajate is typically *serrano*, with a Moslem watchtower and narrow streets surrounded by olive groves and vineyards. A short distance from the main road just after Atajate, Jimera de Líbar has a parish church belltower which, unmistakably, started life as a minaret, an adaptation engineered by the reconquering Christians throughout southern Spain as they tore down the bulk of the mosques during their conquests.

Benadalid

Benadalid, some three miles further south, was once set on the very border between Christian and Moslem empires and the old fortress at the edge of the town saw much bloody fighting over the centuries. Now, like many old castles which have lost their former purpose, it houses the town cemetery.

Gaucin, once a garrison town for the Romans, has the ruins of the Castillo del Aguila which was occupied by determined Moslem forces until 1485, only seven years before the final Reconquest of Spain by the Christians with the fall of Granada. It was here, in 1305, during one of the incessant border disputes that one of the region's great heroes, Guzmán el Bueno, met briefly in our excursion to Santiponce near Seville, died of wounds received in a skirmish.

Jimena de la Frontera

Jimena de la Frontera, which soon appears as a white line in the distance, is one of the larger towns of the sierra. The castle is well preserved and from its heights one can, on a clear day, see Gibraltar and the coast of Morocco. There is no road access; the visitor must climb the steep streets as far as he can by car, then complete the journey on foot. It is not for the fainthearted on a sweltering summer day, though the locals think nothing of it.

The driver will be fortunate if he has not yet had to swerve to avoid odd lumps of bark which invariably find their way onto the roads around Jimena. These are not stray products from a firewood factory, but the raw material of an important local industry – cork production. From bark stripped from local cork oaks come the corks which stop millions of bottles of Spanish wine annually. The method of production can be seen along the roadside at the next diversion on the journey, the road to Castellar de la Frontera which bears to the right shortly after the new town of Nuevo Castellar. The trees are periodically relieved of a section of their bark, which is rolled from the trunk rather like a window blind, and then left to recover for several years before the process is repeated. Partially stripped oaks are curious objects; the lower part of the trunk is black and smooth while the upper retains the familiar rugged appearance of oak bark.

Castellar de la Frontera

Castellar is a town within a castle, the whole set above a dammed lake in a location which deserves better care than it currently receives from the authorities. Behind the city walls lies a warren of small streets which once formed a complete community of homes and shops. Today many of the locals have left for Nuevo Castellar, its modern conveniences being thought more comfortable than the picturesque remoteness of the original settlement. A handful remain; scrubbed iron grills and bright pots of geraniums mark their presence. They have, at the time of writing, been joined by a band of bohemian foreigners at least some of whom seem intent on turning Castellar into some 1960s-style hippy community. A degree of restoration work has begun, but the authorities still seem unsure quite what to make of this most unusual castle. It remains worth a visit for the views alone, but do not expect the trim appearance or facilities of the average pueblo blanco.

The land is now lower and more even, with a varied agriculture. Fields of fighting bulls graze next to acres of sunflowers, before the Mediterranean coast is reached at San Roque. This small town was created by refugees fleeing the British occupation of Gibraltar in 1704. Franco's foolish closure of the border in 1969 blighted the local economy; its reopening in 1985 has only partially eased the poverty of the town.

Here you join the N340 Cádiz to Málaga highway, but well past its busiest and most notorious section between Torremolinos and Estepona. The road leads into Algeciras, the bustling port town from which ferries serve North Africa and the Canary Islands. It is fashionable to dismiss Algeciras as unworthy of a visit. There is nothing of moment to see, but the restaurants are reasonable and the British-owned Reina Cristina hotel, with its fine gardens and views across the bay to Gibraltar, retains something of the atmosphere it once had in the days when the Rock's gentry used it as their social gathering point in Spain.

Lunch in Algeciras.

The Straits of Gibraltar mark the western limits of the Mediterranean. After Algeciras, there are dramatic views across to Morocco, the best being from the Mirador del Estrecho.

Tarifa

The southernmost point of Spain is the small town of Tarifa, an ancient port which is more Moroccan in feel than Spanish. Behind the horseshoe arch which marks the old city's main land entrance lies a tightly-packed community living in streets reminiscent of the alleys of North Africa. The old town and the modern motor car do not mix; leave your vehicle in one of the broad roads which border the town centre and make the short walk on foot.

Most things of note about Tarifa can be seen from the street Guzmán El Bueno which runs past the castle to the old walls where the locals sit in the evening and gaze at the Moroccan coast a few miles away. The castle is where the famous Guzmán earned his renown. Besieged by Moslem forces, his attackers dragged one of the soldier's sons, who was held by them, to the front of the castle where his father, on the ramparts, was told that the youth would die unless the Christians surrendered. Guzmán's response was to throw down his own dagger from the tower and walk away. The unfortunate youth was killed, but Tarifa survived the siege, and Guzmán's family was showered with praise and gifts from the Christian monarchy. A descendant, one of the Dukes of Medina Sidonia, was less successful in martial matters; he was unfortunate enough to lead the Spanish Armada against Britain.

Guzmán's act is commemorated by a statue in the park next to the castle, which depicts him about to throw the dagger. The tower on the east of the city walls, reached by following the street named after the hero, is reputed to be the place where the incident occurred.

Costa de la Luz

After Tarifa, the Atlantic brings a change in the climate. The air becomes crisper and there is an unmistakable clarity to the sky which has lost its Mediterranean vapours. The Spanish call the section of coast from Tarifa to the border with Portugal the Costa de la Luz, the Coast of Light. For the foreign traveller it is one of the great undiscovered regions of Spain. The beaches are, in the main, superb, as the golden sands which stretch west of Tarifa show, even from the car. There is but one drawback for the average tourist: a near constant wind which blows off the sea. These conditions, however, have made the area a near paradise for windsurfers who flock from all over Europe to spend their days zooming across the blue waters at breakneck speeds; they have also very effectively prevented the development of this part of the coast as a conventional resort area.

A turning marked to Bolonia leads down to another, less windy bay, where there are a few hostels and restaurants and the remains of a Roman community in which the imaginative may see fish salting pits, temples and a forum. The ruins are, in truth, disappointing for most, but the wild, remote location is idyllic.

Returning to the main road, a few miles north there is another turning to the small fishing village of Zahara de los Atunes. As its name implies, this is a tuna fishing region. The counters of bars and restaurants invariably offer *atún* in a variety of ways, as well as a local white fish, *pez de limón,* which is a speciality. Zahara has an excellent beach and facilities, including one luxury hotel. The local atmosphere and lack of development are likely to convert those who would otherwise abhor a beach holiday, something which can be said of many of the resorts on the Costa de la Luz.

There is little more to Zahara than a few modest lines of fishermen's cottages and the occasional new apartment block. But I suspect it would be a strong contender to win any contest to find Spain's most unspoilt seaside community. The taverns have the authentic touch of true fishing inns... hooks and nets adorn the walls and hunks of blood-red tuna sit in cabinets waiting for hungry customers. It is a sobering thought that several of the better known Spanish resorts, such as Marbella and Torremolinos, were little more than this some forty years ago.

Overnight in Zahara de los Atunes.

ACCOMMODATION

Most facilities in Zahara close between November and January. However, the village is becoming more popular with visitors, and some establishments are changing their opening habits.

Atlanterra Palacio
Bahia de la Plata
Zahara de los Atunes
Tel: 432700/430973

Luxurious Sol chain hotel with views to Morocco, two miles from Zahara. The Atlanterra is decorated in Moorish style and was voted Spain's most beautiful hotel in 1984. The Atlanterra is extraordinarily sumptuous, to the point of incongruity in this little-developed part of the Spanish coast. Hotel services are expensive, and the staff, on my visit, distinctly unwelcoming.

Closed November to January
Rooms: 284
Facilities: outdoor pool, tennis, beach, terrace, disco
Credit cards: American Express, Diner's Club, Eurocard, Visa
Rating *****

Antonio
Zahara de los Atunes
Tel: 431241

Comfortable, cheap accommodation on the edge of the village. Booking recommended.

Closed late November and December
Rooms: 11
Credit cards: American Express, Diner's Club, Eurocard, Visa
Rating **

Hostal Castro
Zahara de los Atunes
Tel: 430248

Modest, inexpensive rooms attached to a reasonable restaurant in the heart of the village, close to the beach.

Open all year
Credit cards: Visa
Rooms: 24
Rating **

EATING OUT

Bar Marisquería Porfirio
Plaza Tamarón
Zahara de los Atunes
Tel: 430348

Zahara's most popular fish tavern, with excellent lobster and *pez de limón*. Tables outside look out onto the small village square and are rapidly occupied on summer evenings. Reservations are essential for Sundays.

Open every day, closed December
Credit cards: American Express, Diner's Club, Eurocard, Visa
Rating ***

El Atún Alegre
Plaza Tamarón
Zahara de los Atunes

Friendly modern bar opposite the Porfirio with tapas of fresh tuna and Spanish sausage and a quiet patio. English-speaking owner.

Open every day
No credit cards
Rating **

Reina Cristina
Paseo de la Conferencia
Algeciras
Tel: 602622

International cuisine from the Trust House Forte group in the smart dining room of Algeciras's most plush hotel.

Open all year
Credit cards: American Express, Diner's Club, Eurocard, Visa
Rating ****

Iris
San Bernardo 1 (in hotel Octavio building which can be seen from the Tourist Information centre on the waterfront)
Algeciras
Tel: 655806

Popular, functional local restaurant in an uninspiring location, serving local dishes, including the seafood casserole, *zarzuela*; mussels in sauce, *mejillones marinara*, and red mullet, *salmonetes*.

Open every day
Credit cards: American Express, Diner's Club, Visa
Rating **

ALGECIRAS: USEFUL INFORMATION
Tourist office: Avda de la Marina
                      Tel: 600911
Population: 86,042
Facilities: ferries to North Africa

ZAHARA DE LOS ATUNES
Population: 1,891

Arcos de la Frontera

DAY 7

From Zahara de los Atunes to Arcos de la Frontera via Vejer de la Frontera and Medina Sidonia, about 50 miles.

The route leads inland, via the fishing port of Barbate and the hill town of Vejer de la Frontera, to one of the most picturesque mountain communities of western Andalucia, Arcos de la Frontera.

Overnight at Arcos de la Frontera.

Route shown p. 75.

Map references
Zahara de los Atunes	36° 09´N 5° 51´W
Vejer de la Frontera	36° 18´N 5° 58´W
Medina Sidonia	36° 28´N 5° 57´W
Arcos de la Frontera	36° 45´N 5° 50´W

Breakfast in Zahara de los Atunes.

An early morning start will bring you to Arcos de la Frontera for lunch. There are no notable restaurants between Zahara and Arcos, though you will find adequate tapas in cafés in both Vejer and Medina Sidonia.

From Zahara a seafront road leads left after the bridge to the unremarkable fishing town of Barbate de Franco and then turns inland with a diversion, just before the N340, to the hillside community of Vejer de la Frontera.

Vejer de la Frontera

This town of narrow streets and ancient houses, some of them unexpectedly large and sumptuous, changed hands several times in the conflicts of the Reconquest. Little of Arabic influence remains, save a local tale that, even into this century, the women of the town wore Moorish *cobijadas*, dark robes which covered them head to foot. The *cobijada* is never seen today, and this story may well be an apocryphal one for the tourist books.

Few visitors bother to make the minor detour into Vejer, which is a shame since the whitewashed medieval streets, with their flowers and ironwork, are the very picture of rural Andalucia. A brisk walk to the castle at the summit of the town is rewarded with views of the mountains, the Cape of Trafalgar towards Cádiz, and south, on a good day, across the straits to North Africa.

Medina Sidonia

From Vejer a minor road runs directly inland, through rich farmland, to Medina Sidonia. The turning lies between the two exits from Vejer; if you choose the most northerly one you will need to take the N340 towards Algeciras for a little way before finding it.

Traces of Arabic influence are by no means uncommon in Andalucian place names, but Medina Sidonia can boast a new variation on this theme. The first part of its name is Arabic, while the latter comes from the Phoenician town of Sidon. It was this town that became the dukedom of the Guzmán family, the descendants of the hero El Bueno of Tarifa. The dukes of Medina Sidonia were active participants on the Spanish stage for several centuries; the Spanish Armada and the colonisation of the new world were just two of the ventures in which they played important roles.

Their legacy of fame and fortune is reflected in the town today, with its rich, if rather crumbling buildings, and air of genteel decay. The car can take you into the very heart of Medina, following the signs for the Castillo and the church of Santa María la Coronada. There is a small cobbled square at the summit in front of the church and ample parking space. Medina is best explored from here as far as the very foot of the town where there is a handsome Moslem entrance gate.

The church has been built among the ruins of a castle that preceded it, and is of a Gothic style which falls just short of ostentation. In the clear air, with swifts and more colourful birds wheeling in the sky and views across to Cádiz, one can forgive the occasional extra flourish of masonry. Inside there is a *retablo*, or altarpiece, which is regarded as an important piece of Andalucian art, but the light is poor and, at the time of writing, the inevitable restoration work is under way. The interior is enjoyable for its feeling of space and the raggle taggle collection of artefacts from many centuries which seem to have found their way into the church. Foreign visitors are still sufficiently rare to bring a genuine smile of welcome from the church warden on duty, and he can tell colourful tales of many of the paintings and carvings for those with the Spanish to follow.

A tower from the earlier fortification adjoins the church and on it a plaque commemorates one of the many bloody deeds of Pedro the Cruel, the now familiar Spanish monarch with a record that makes Shakespeare's Richard III look like Edward the Confessor. It was here that Pedro's wife, Blanche of Bourbon, was murdered on the orders of her husband. Here too Pedro's men also murdered the mistress of his dead father, Leonor de Guzmán – you may see how this name is never far from the pages of Spanish history. The cruel king's deed was revenged by Leonor's sons who usurped and murdered him, founding a new royal dynasty.

Arcos de la Frontera

From Medina cross the C440 Jerez to Algeciras highway and continue inland, following the signs for Arcos, perhaps the most dramatic of all the pueblos blancos, as you may appreciate watching the craggy outline of the town appear ahead, a spectacular collection of church, castle and white houses set on the edge of a cliff which overlooks the lazy sweep of the Guadalete river which rises near the inland Zahara, passed on our way from Carmona to Ronda, and reaches the sea at Cádiz.

Lunch in Arcos de la Frontera.

Arcos is an unspoilt delight rising from the plain of the Guadalete, with panoramic views, an excellent parador, and winding streets and alleyways of brilliant white houses that stay in the memory long after some of the grander sights of Andalucia have faded. The streets were never meant for the motor car, and a degree of patience is required by anyone seeking to find the centre – that is the summit – of the town, the Plaza de España, site of the parador and an esplanade with views of the surrounding region. The simplest thing is to look out for the signs to the parador and cling to them for dear life, round tight corners, narrow alleys blocked by bread delivery vans, and tribes of pensioners out for their daily constitutional. The police-men of Arcos appear to have little to do but work out how to fit a modern traffic flow into a medieval town of labyrinthine alleys, and they carry out the task with surprising good humour.

When you finally turn into the Plaza, a car park attendant will guide you to a space – and expect a small tip. And here the car may be abandoned, for the parador and the hotel El Convento are only yards away.

Arcos has its fair share of monuments. The church in the Plaza, Santa María, is late Gothic with traces of early Moslem workmanship, and its rival church, San Pedro, identifiable by the taller, baroque belltower, has a lesser collection of historic artefacts. But the best way to appreciate Arcos is simply to wander its old streets, winding past palaces and more humble homes set cheek by jowl, shining brightly in the sun.

Overnight in Arcos de la Frontera.

ACCOMMODATION

Parador Casa del Corregidor
Plaza de España
Arcos de la Frontera
Tel: 700500

Restful modern parador in a quiet square. Somewhat lacking in atmosphere, but the rooms are comfortable and the dining room reliable.
Essential to reserve your room in advance.

Open all year
Rooms: 24
Credit cards: American Express, Diner's Club, Eurocard, Visa
Rating ****

El Convento
Maldonado 2
Arcos de la Frontera
Tel: 702333

Tiny private hotel and restaurant set close to the Plaza de España and
opposite the main market building. Quiet, comfortable rooms with a helpful staff. Advance booking is highly recommended.

Open all year
Rooms: 4
Credit cards: Visa
Rating **

EATING OUT

El Convento (see above)

Local specialities, including hot garlic soup, *ajo a la comendora*, and wild
rabbit, feature on a changing menu. There are no fine restaurants beyond

91

this and the parador dining room, at the time of writing, but the usual local dishes and tapas can be found in more modest establishments.

MEDINA SIDONIA: USEFUL INFORMATION

Tourist office:	Tourist information is available from the church of Santa María la Coronada

ARCOS DE LA FRONTERA

Tourist office:	Tourist information is available from the parador
Population:	24,902

Medina Sidonia

DAY 8

Arcos de la Frontera to Jerez de la Frontera, about 20 miles.

The sherry capital of Jerez de la Frontera is only a brief drive away and, by booking in advance, the visitor can see round one of the famous *bodegas*. Jerez is also notable for its fine restaurants, love of horsemanship, and several historic buildings.

Overnight in Jerez de la Frontera.

Route shown p. 75.

Map references

Arcos de la Frontera	36° 45´N 5° 50´W
Jerez de la Frontera	36° 42´N 6° 08´W

Breakfast in Arcos de la Frontera.

Jerez de la Frontera

The patron saint of Jerez de la Frontera is the Roman martyr Dionisio, which seems appropriate given that his namesake was the ancient god of revelry. But all is not as it seems here, and Jerez is far from dionysian in character. Like many towns associated with the manufacture of alcoholic drink – Bordeaux and Rheims to name but two – Jerez maintains an air of serious, wealthy dignity, as if to prove to the world that its dedication to viticulture is no frivolous thing in spite of the obvious side effects of its most famous product.

The route is a short and easy one, consisting of some 20 miles of winding road on the N342 as it heads for the coast. The next three days cover very little in the way of miles, but a wealth of different yet connected social and cultural emotions in the relatively small area bounded by Jerez, to the east, Cádiz to the west, and Sanlúcar de Barrameda on the banks of the Guadalquivir to the north.

Jerez, perhaps because of its long connection with the British, perhaps because of its natural economic advantages, has a cosmopolitan atmosphere about it. The restaurants are markedly more adventurous than those of neighbouring towns, the hotels, usually, try a little harder, and one is conscious of an effort to maintain for the world the picture which the average Jerez gentleman, be he car park attendant or sherry baron, has of himself and his city.

Lunch in Jerez de la Frontera.

Sherry, important as it is, is only one facet in this image. But it is to the *bodegas* that visitors are inevitably drawn in the first instance, and with good reason for tours are usually well organised and interesting, and, of course, culminate in a generous sampling of the various brands available. All five large houses – Gonzalez Byass, Sandeman, Williams, Domecq and Harvey – have *bodegas* in the city as well as large estates outside. It is best to make an appointment beforehand, even if it is only a phone call from your hotel around 9am, so that you may be found a place in a tour with an English-speaking guide.

94

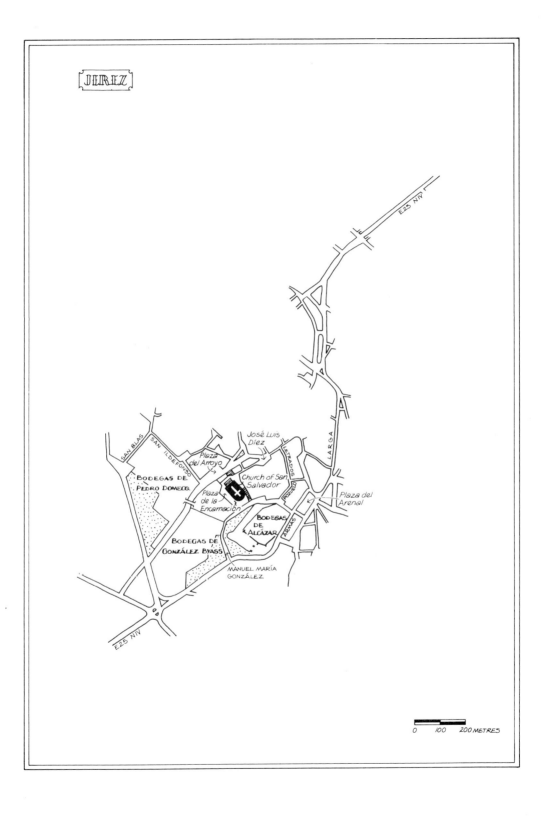

JEREZ

San Blas
San Ildefonso
José Luis Díez
Plaza del Arroyo
BODEGAS DE PEDRO DOMECQ
Church of San Salvador
Plaza de la Encarnación
LETRADOS
POZUELO
LARGA
Plaza del Arenal
BODEGAS DE ALCÁZAR
ARMAS
BODEGAS DE GONZÁLEZ BYASS
MANUEL MARÍA GONZÁLEZ
E25 NIV
E25 NIV

0   100   200 METRES

There is little to choose between the tours, though Byass, with its enormous *bodega* behind the Alcázar which encompasses a few original, preserved streets of the old city, is the closest to the centre of the town. Its royal *bodega* was designed by Eiffel, barrels signed by celebrities from Martin Luther King to Franco are on show (the latter's signature covered in glass to prevent those with long memories rubbing it out). Finally, there are the Byass resident wild mice, first trained more than 50 years ago to creep out of cracks in the floor, then climb a small ladder for a sip of sherry. The ritual is performed daily with some success at the beginning of the visits. Later tours will often find the mice are, by now, somewhat comatose and unwilling to creep out from their lairs, at which point a mildly embarassed guide will hand round pictures of them in action to prove the whole thing is not a fairy story.

As with all the *bodegas*, the pretence is maintained that there is only one decent house in the whole world and it is the one that you have been fortunate enough to select for your visit. So, at Byass, you will be told that there is really only one great *fino* and that is the famous Tio Pepe. While at Domecq the same pride will be shown in the equally popular La Ina.

There are four principal types of sherry, *fino*, dry and pale in colour and the most popular for domestic consumption, *amontillado*, still dry but with more body and darker in colour, *oloroso*, a medium sherry, and finally *dulce*, the cream of the British grandmother's parlour. Britain is by far the largest single importer of sherry in the world, and English names abound throughout the Jerez *bodegas*. As is so often the case, the drink is tailored to overseas tastes for export, in this case sweetened greatly, even under the same name. So an *amontillado* destined for Britain may be made sweeter than that sold as the same brand in Spain. Few Spanish touch the sweetest *dulce* at all, and a number are frankly amazed that anyone does – just as the solid citizens of Cognac scratch their heads in puzzlement that Britain's favourite brandy is three star stuff which they would never allow past the kitchen condiments cabinet.

Sherry is a fortified wine produced by the *solera* process. This entails the movement of wine from nursery barrels into a final 'mother' barrel from which it is taken, a third at a time, for bottling. All sherries are blended which means that there are no vintage years and, in theory, consistent quality for a brand whatever the harvest. To summarise the complexities of the *solera* process in one paragraph is impossible. It is an art and a ritual – two things which the Jerez gentleman loves, as one can see when he begins to play with the *venencia*, the long-handled container used to draw sherry from a cask, and drops the wine into the glass without spilling a drop. Naturally, *fino* may be drunk at any time of day, with food or without, and is a substantial improvement on ordinary white wine, even at meals. Asking for a glass of white table wine anywhere near Jerez is to prompt uproar, but the Jerez gentleman will, of course, normally understand *fino* for *vino* and hand you sherry instead.

Red wine is an acceptable alternative drink if you must, and white might just arrive at the table if you insist on a vintage from Rioja, a region of similar temperament to Jerez. The harvest in Jerez is celebrated each September with a lively fiesta in which costumed grape gatherers parade through the streets.

The two other obsessions of Jerez are horses and bulls. Equestrian skill here is taken for granted, in much the same way that a child learns to ride a bicycle. At the great horse fair in May the sale of livestock plays something of a minor part. Men and women parade on horseback in full dress costume, and there is great competition for the prizes in racing, trotting and dressage. The *Royal School of Andalucian Equestrian Arts* – no mere riding school, you see – demonstrates these impressive skills to the public every Thursday at noon. Every other day, bar Sundays and holidays, the stables are open from 11am to 1.30pm. Advance booking is advisable for the performances.

The bulls of Jerez roam vast estates seen from the roadside, herded from horseback. They provide Spain's finest fighting creatures, with family lines nurtured from pugnacious generation to generation. Several of the famous sherry families also own country estates which are largely concerned with breeding for the ring. The raising of pedigree bulls is a task for the gentleman, not that of a mere farmer.

The original Moslem fortress of the Alcázar remains, with a pleasant park nearby. It was the fall of the Moslem forces which gave Jerez Dionisio as its patron saint, for the Christian victory occurred on the saint's day. The church of San Dionisio was built largely by Moslem craftsmen, making it a good example of the *mudéjar* style. The dominant place of worship is the

Collegiate Church of San Salvador, an imposing and massive construction which combines a variety of architectural styles, from *mudéjar* to Roman.

One curiosity which may be seen three miles outside the city is the handsome Carthusian Monastery currently being restored. This was once the home of the famous collection of Zurbarán paintings now housed in Cádiz. The neglect of years is obvious but, at the time of writing, it seems likely that the building will be restored in its entirety and opened to the public.

Overnight in Jerez de la Frontera.

ACCOMMODATION

Jerez
Alvaro Domecq 35
Jerez de la Frontera
Tel: 300600

Modern, luxurious hotel a mile from the centre of Jerez, in beautiful gardens set back from the busy main road to Seville. Deservedly popular with foreign visitors, and far superior to any other hotel in Jerez.

Open all year
Rooms: 121
Credit cards: American Express, Diner's Club, Eurocard, Visa
Rating ****

Capele
Corredera 58
Jerez de la Frontera
Tel: 340700

Unmemorable, largely business hotel close to the centre.

Open all year
Rooms: 30
Credit cards: American Express, Diner's Club, Eurocard, Visa
Rating **

EATING OUT

Gaitán
Gaitán 3
Jerez de la Frontera
Tel: 345859

Behind an unassuming facade in a narrow street close to the centre of the town lies one of the best restaurants in the region. The award-winning Gaitán serves a wide range of dishes, local and from other parts of Spain, in a small, decorated dining room. Most customers are Jerez businessmen and their families. Dishes range from smoked pork chop with chestnut sauce to the Catalan speciality of partridge with chocolate and an excellent Sevillian duck with olives. Highly recommended.

Closed Sunday nights
Credit cards: American Express, Diner's Club, Eurocard, Visa
Rating ***

El Bosque
Alvaro Domecq 26
Jerez de la Frontera
Tel: 303333

Expensive, largely international cuisine in a lovely park near the Hotel Jerez. An ideal setting for sherry baron power lunches... perhaps a bit formal for the average tourist lunch.

Open all year
Credit cards: American Express, Diner's Club, Eurocard, Visa
Rating ****

Venta Antonio
Ctra. de Sanlúcar de Barrameda
Jerez de la Frontera
Tel: 330535

Just outside Jerez, on the road to Sanlúcar, this is an enormous country house restaurant serving superb fish dishes: fresh lobster, langoustines, monkfish, and sea bass, all displayed for the many local customers who return time after time. The place has a tremendous local following and is overrun with families on Sundays – hence the playground facilities.

Closed Mondays in winter
Credit cards: American Express, Diner's Club, Eurocard, Visa
Rating ****

**JEREZ DE LA FRONTERA:
USEFUL INFORMATION**

Tourist office:	Alameda Christina 7
	Tel: 331150/331162
Population:	176,238
Facilities:	airport, bullring, motor racetrack

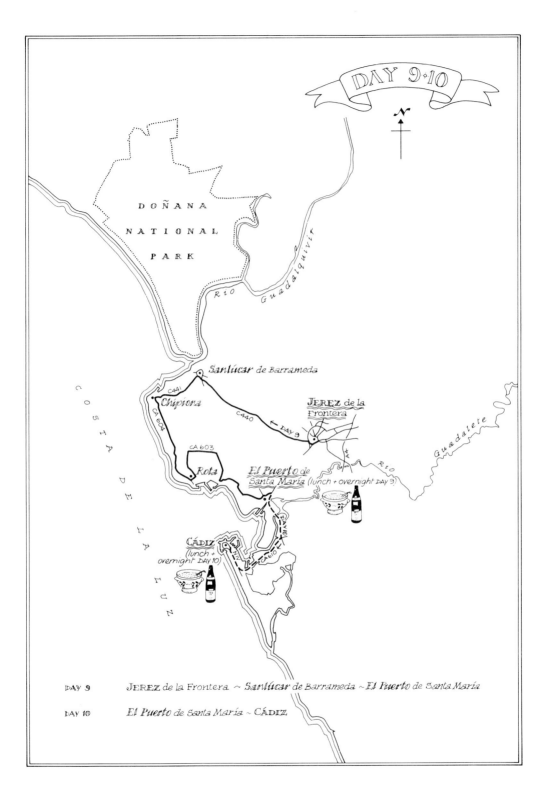

DAY 9 • 10

DOÑANA
NATIONAL
PARK

Rio Guadalquivir

COSTA DE LA LUZ

Sanlúcar de Barrameda

CA 441
Chipiona
CA 604
C-440
← DAY 9

JEREZ de la
Frontera

CA 603

Rota

El Puerto de
Santa María (lunch + overnight DAY 9)

Rio Guadalete

Rio

CÁDIZ
(lunch +
overnight DAY 10)

Rio

DAY 9   JEREZ de la Frontera ~ Sanlúcar de Barrameda ~ El Puerto de Santa María

DAY 10   El Puerto de Santa María ~ CÁDIZ

Sanlúcar

DAY 9

Jerez de la Frontera to El Puerto de Santa María via Sanlúcar de Barrameda, about 45 miles.

The journey continues to Sanlúcar de Barrameda, a small fishing town at the mouth of the Guadalquivir and home of the sherry variant *manzanilla*, and then moves south to the old port of El Puerto de Santa María, little known to the foreign visitor but famous throughout Spain for its food and wine. Its ancient quarter was once the home of Spain's pioneering mariners, among them Columbus and Amerigo Vespucci.

Overnight in El Puerto de Santa María.

Route shown p. 101.

Map references

Jerez de la Frontera	36° 42´N 6° 08´W
Sanlúcar de Barrameda	36° 45´N 6° 22´W
Chipiona	36° 43´N 6° 28´W
Rota	36° 37´N 6° 22´W
El Puerto de Santa María	36° 36´N 6° 15´W

Breakfast in Jerez de la Frontera.

This is a somewhat circuitous route from Jerez to the pleasurable town known to the whole of Spain as 'El Puerto', but a more interesting one than the fast main road which joins the two directly. The turning is close to the Byass *bodega*, running past the fine restaurant of Venta Antonio, through vineyards and wheat fields to the town of Sanlúcar de Barrameda, situated at the mouth of the Guadalquivir, now a broad, powerful sweep of water unrecognisable from the lively little stream that rises more than 200 miles away, as the crow flies, in the Sierra de Cazorla to the east.

Sanlúcar de Barrameda

The suburbs of Sanlúcar are modern and uninteresting, and the casual visitor could easily come to believe that this was little more than a pleasant beach resort of comparatively recent origin. In fact, it is an ancient and distinguished town, as venerable, in its own small way, as Jerez, El Puerto or Cádiz. The old town, set back from the modern beach development, has several notable buildings and the customary tangle of little streets which the visitor will by now expect of this part of Andalucia. There is a handsome 16th-century church, with the curious name of Nuestra Senora de la O, and an equally interesting palace of the Dukes of Medina Sidonia, descendants of the hero Guzmán, met at Santiponce and Tarifa.

To the Andalucian, Sanlúcar is famous for two more worldly items, the version of *fino* known as *manzanilla*, and the local catch of large prawns, *langostinos*. Manzanilla is made in much the same way as *fino*, and many of the *bodegas* you will see in the town are owned by houses from Jerez. The drink has a distinct, added dryness and sharpness, however, and will appeal to anyone who finds even the *fino* of Tio Pepe or La Ina a little too cloying. This extra, salty bite is often attributed to the marine air of the town, though there is doubtless a more practical explanation if one could extract it from the *bodega* owners. For many years *manzanilla* was rarely exported, but recently, with the growing fashion for things Spanish, it has been picked up by foreign buyers and at least one British supermarket chain now markets its own brand, supplied directly from the *bodegas* of Sanlúcar.

The *langostino* is a beast greatly admired by the Spanish, either *cocido* (boiled) or *a la plancha* (grilled). The brown-striped beauties of Sanlúcar are known for their flavour and freshness... and for their price. Just one *langostino* will usually cost more than a single oyster, and it is not the most filling of creatures. One must always carry the suspicion that an inferior, perhaps frozen, alternative has been substituted too, for there are great profits to be made from these modest little creatures. Fish stalls inevitably label those from Sanlúcar, differentiating them from the rest of the bunch, but seafood bars may be less scrupulous. Nevertheless, a glass of *manzanilla* and one *langostino* in one of the many seafood bars may be thought to be pretty mandatory here, but there is a greater variety of restaurants in El Puerto de Santa María, so I would suggest that you take lunch there.

It is from Sanlúcar that one may depart for one of the more unusual excursions of the area, into the most secluded parts of the national park of Doñana on the far bank of the Guadalquivir. Half day trips by jeep are organised throughout the year, but advance booking is essential (the tourist office can advise on bookings). No private cars are allowed into Doñana, an area rich in birds and reptiles and well administered by the Spanish authorities. Flamingoes, wild boar, fallow deer, wild horses, and a vast population of ducks and geese inhabit the coastal dunes and fresh-water lagoons of the park.

There is a slow, but pleasant coastal road from Sanlúcar to El Puerto via Chipiona and Rota. The former is a modern resort town, the latter rather older but dominated by the vast American air force base which is the source of some controversy within Spain. American cars and the odd road-side bar offering Tennessee style spare ribs mark the American presence. Yet one rarely meets residents of the base in neighbouring towns, and El Puerto itself, though only ten miles from the Rota runways, shows no sign of being a satellite town of the US air force.

El Puerto de Santa María

The casual visitor to this region rarely comes to El Puerto, preferring the better known sights of Jerez and Cádiz. Yet to the Spanish, the town is the greatest attraction of the area, for its delightful casual atmosphere, the sights, the beaches and the variety and quality of its restaurants. A day out in El Puerto is a holiday for any resident of Cádiz, Jerez or even Seville... which should be a sufficiently good recommendation for any of us.

All the great names of Spanish maritime history, including Columbus and Amerigo Vespucci, who gave his name to America, knew the lively streets of El Puerto intimately. They lived here, searching for backers and competent mariners to man their explorations. The Santa María, the ship in which Columbus sailed to the New World hoping to find a western passage to the Indies, was built in an El Puerto yard.

Lunch in El Puerto.

The old town begins just behind the waterfront, close to where the *Vapor* daily steamer service to Cádiz departs. If you have not booked a place at the Hotel Atlántico in Cádiz it is perfectly possible to use El Puerto as a base for visiting both cities, with the *Vapor*'s 45-minute journey across the bay as the link. But the hotel facilities in El Puerto do not match those of the excellent Atlántico.

The principal sights can be seen in half a day. Begin in Palacios, near the waterfront, walking into the old town in the direction of the imposing main church, the Iglesia Mayor Prioral, which can be seen at the top of the street. It is a fetching building, the best side being the Renaissance face seen from Palacios. Turning left at the church, along Santa Lucia, brings one eventually to the magisterial Plaza de Toros which seems of such a size that it is out of place in a town with a population of fewer than 60,000 residents. Yet the century-old ring has a certain prestige, accommodating 15,000 spectators and ranking third in importance in Spain, after Madrid and Valencia. From the bullring, head back towards the seafront, along Los Moros then Fernan Caballero, stopping at the Osborne *bodega* if you would like to visit another sherry house, and one which is somewhat less formal than those of Jerez. Smaller *bodegas* lurk down narrow sidestreets and welcome foreign visitors in what is an exceptionally friendly Andalucian town. The smell of sherry hangs over parts of El Puerto all year long.

Turning left at the Plaza del Polvorista brings one behind the 13th-century Castle of San Marcos, and one may follow the walls of this much restored, somewhat fairytale red fortress round in a clockwise direction to the Plaza del Cristóbal Colón, so named because Columbus – Cristóbal Colón in Spanish – stayed in one of the houses there. The castle is in private hands and closed to the public, which is a great shame since it contains many items of interest.

Beyond the *Vapor* point lies the Ribera del Marisco, where several identical and equally superb fish restaurants are situated. These are casual places – shellfish, plain or fried, and local fish are bought from a separate stall and then carried by the customer to a table where drinks can be bought. The quality is as high as you will find anywhere in Andalucia and the atmosphere friendly and relaxed.

Behind Ribera del Marisco is another old quarter of quiet plazas and pretty, narrow streets which, throughout the evening, become crowded with visiting Spanish families promenading before a meal or tapas in the local bars. It is hard not to be enchanted by El Puerto. The town's one drawback is the shortage of good, central hotels.

Overnight in El Puerto de Santa María.

ACCOMMODATION

Los Cántaros
Curva 2
El Puerto de Santa María
Tel: 864240

Middling comfort close to the Ribero del Marisco, and noise could prove a problem.

Open all year
Rooms: 39
Credit cards: American Express, Diner's Club, Eurocard, Visa
Rating **

Hotel Monasterio de San Miguel
Larga 27
El Puerto de Santa María
Tel: 861200

Excellent, central hotel, located in a former monastery and refurbished at great expense, with a swimming pool and gardens.

Rooms: 150
Credit cards: American Express, Diner's Club, Eurocard, Visa
Rating ****

El Caballo Blanco
Ctra. de Cádiz
El Puerto de Santa María
Tel: 863745

Part of the Melia chain, which means predictable modern comfort, in this case a little over a mile from El Puerto on the main road to Cádiz. A compromise, but a reliable one which could be used as a base for both El Puerto and Cádiz.

Open all year
Rooms: 94
Facilities: outdoor pool
Credit cards: American Express, Diner's Club, Eurocard, Visa
Rating ***

EATING OUT

Alboronia
Santo Domingo 24
El Puerto de Santa María
Tel: 851609

Unquestionably one of the finest restaurants in Andalucia. The Alboronia occupies a fine mansion in the old town and represents some of the best aspects of modern Spanish cuisine. In addition to the à la carte menu, two fixed price meals are on offer, the larger recommended for gargantuan appetites only. Fresh salmon with old *amontillado* sauce, oysters, leg of lamb, and monkfish in champagne sauce, each course served with an appropriate fine wine, typify the cuisine, which is light and imaginative. A more sophisticated dinner is hard to find, even in Seville. The prices are high by Spanish standards, but few will complain.

Closed Sundays
Credit cards: American Express, Diner's Club, Eurocard, Visa
Rating ****

El Horreo Asturiano
Misericordia 9
El Puerto de Santa María
Tel: 859856

Fine food, principally from the province of Asturias. Try the piquant *Cabrales* cheese, *fabada* casserole of beans and sausage, tiny eels *angulas*, and an excellent roast leg of lamb, Castilian style.

Closed Sunday nights
Credit cards: American Express, Diner's Club, Eurocard, Visa
Rating ***

El Resbaladero
Aurora 1
El Puerto de Santa María
Tel: 856853

Housed in the old fish market, the Resbaladero offers conventional Spanish cuisine of high standards, usually served with the world weariness often seen in restaurants of its ilk. Oysters, salmon, swordfish, kid and pickled partridge are appetising, and there is a popular tapas bar for those who just want a snack.

Open every day
Credit cards: Visa
Rating **

Ribera del Marisco

There is little to choose between the first-rate seafood restaurants in the street. All serve a range of shellfish, crabs and fried fish from the counter, and have a bar attached. Portions are bought according to weight; shellfish, notably Sanlúcar's *langostinos*, can be expensive.

EL PUERTO DE SANTA MARIA: USEFUL INFORMATION		
Tourist office:	Calle Guadalete Tel: 863145	
Population:	57,000	
Facilities:	bullring, casino	
SANLUCAR DE BARRAMEDA		
Tourist office:	Baños Tel: 360432/362611	
Population:	50,000	

DAY 10

El Puerto de Santa María to Cádiz, about 18 miles.

A short car journey, or the boat service from El Puerto, takes the visitor to the city of Cádiz, sited on the edge of a promontory overlooking the Atlantic. There one finds a famous art gallery and cathedral, enjoyable walks around the sea walls, and several fine eating places which reflect the city's passion for fish.

Overnight in Cádiz.

Route shown p. 101.

Map references
El Puerto de Santa María   36° 36′N 6° 15′W
Cádiz   36° 32′N 6° 18′W

Breakfast in El Puerto de Santa María.

Leave El Puerto on the main road travelling south, the NIV, signposted for Cádiz, or take a 45-minute steamer trip across the bay.

Cádiz

The old city of Cádiz occupies an exposed promontory at the end of a narrow peninsula surrounded by salt flats. It is a glorious location, virtually encircled by the sea, and the fresh Atlantic air makes Cádiz shine whiter and brighter than any other city in Andalucia. Modern suburbs grow on the approaches from El Puerto, but everything of interest lies within the crowded, narrow streets still bounded by the sea walls.

Cádiz is one of the oldest cities in Spain, the Roman Gades, and the citizens still call themselves Gadetanos as a conscious reminder to all of their breeding. It is a city for walking – a circuit around the sea walls will take under two hours, at a leisurely pace with the occasional pause. Anglers of all ages try their luck with enormous rods over the walls, couples chatter in the tropical park of Genovés, and bathers swim on the small beach of La Caleta, often in the siesta from the office or classroom. There is a large university which supplies the town with its lively academic community.

And a sense of humour too. The British burned and bombarded Cádiz on no fewer than six occasions, the first being Drake's bold singeing of Philip II's beard in 1587. If you buy a copy of the excellent *Diario de Cádiz* daily newspaper, you will find that the author of the astrology column is one Frances Drake...

This independent-minded attitude came to the fore in one of the most famous episodes of recent Spanish history, the declaration in 1812 of a liberal constitution and foundation of a *Cortes* or parliament in rebellion against Napoleon's occupying forces. The wording of the constitution struck a chord among liberals throughout Europe.

When the Spanish king Ferdinand VII, whose cause, among others, it was designed to promote, was restored two years later, he immediately rejected the constitution. Cádiz rebelled against Ferdinand in 1820, taking the king prisoner three years later. The French came to the king's aid and over-

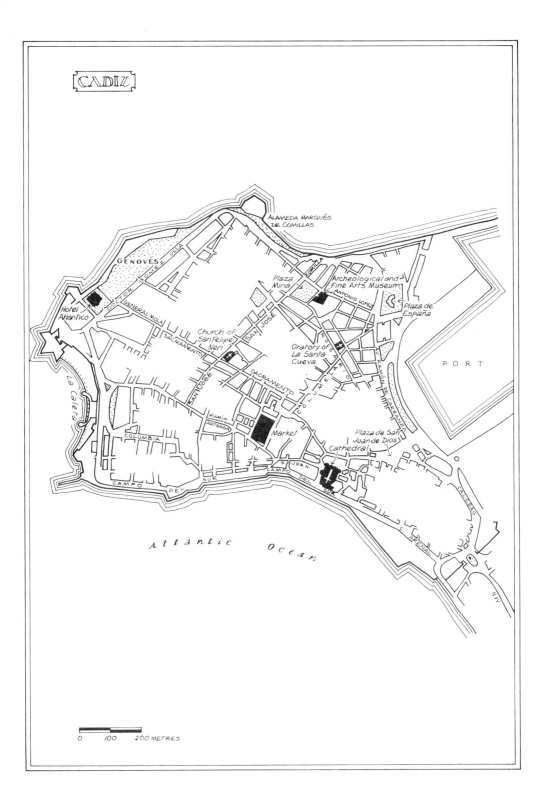

CADIZ

ALAMEDA MARQUÉS
DE COMILLAS

GENOVÉS

Plaza
Mina

Archeological and
Fine Arts Museum

ANTONIO LOPEZ

Plaza de
España

Hotel
Atlantico

GENERAL MOLA

SACRAMENTO

Church of
San Felipe
Neri

Oratory of
La Santa
Cueva

PORT

La Caleta

SAN JOSE

SACRAMENTO

COLUMELA

RAMON DE CARRANZA

SAN JOSE

MARÍA
ARTEAGA

COLUMBIA

Market

Plaza de San
Juan de Dios

CAMPO   DEL   SUR

S. JUAN

Cathedral

CAMPO   DEL   SUR

C. APELAL

CALESAS

NIV

A t l a n t i c   O c e a n

0   100   200 METRES

threw the rebellion. This distinctly Spanish turn of events is a sad and instructive lesson in the nation's politics. It is sobering to think that only in the last decade did Spain achieve a government which was both stable and democratic.

The spirit of rebellion still runs through Cádiz today and, at the right time of year, one can witness the local communist party commemorating the anniversary of the death of Che Guevara. The annual celebrations to mark the declaration of the constitution attract wider support, but in both cases the goal, one suspects, is more enjoyment of yet another open air fiesta rather than some political point.

Cádiz is in a perpetual state of restoration, and it is impossible to predict at any time which sights will be open, and when. The city owns one of the finest collections of paintings in Spain but, and this is a considerable scandal, the best have been removed from public view for more than a year and there is no sign of when they may return – all in the cause of creating new gallery space. A measure of how slowly life moves here may be gained when I say that in March 1987 I was told that the collections would be back on show in July of that year. In July 1988, the same notice warning visitors of their disappearance was fading on the museum wall, and I was told that they might be back on show in 1989 'possibly'.

They include a marvellous – by all accounts – collection of works by the Andalucian artist Zurbarán, better than those by the same artist to be seen in Seville. Many were originally from the Carthusian monastery in Jerez where they might have remained for all the use they have been to the public in recent times. Works by Murillo and Morales are also kept out of view at the time of writing. The rest of the collection of the Fine Arts Museum is of moderate interest, but scarcely worth the premium entry fee of 250 pesetas charged by the authorities. The archeological museum next door to the fine arts museum is, at the time of writing, totally closed for restoration and may even have become history itself by the time it opens.

Both of these frustrating institutions are situated in the Plaza Mina where you will also find a helpful tourist office. It is a pleasant open square with benches where Gadetanos rest in the shade of palm trees during the afternoon, perhaps trying to recall what their great paintings really look like.

The small delicatessen Barreda on the corner of San Jose sells sealed packets of Spanish saffron, *azafrán*, at reasonable prices – ideal gifts for anyone with a culinary bent.

The little street of Zorrilla, which leads from the tourist office to the sea wall, has its pleasures to help the visitor cease fuming about inhospitable monuments. This is a more compact introduction to the pleasures of tapas in Spain than Seville's Triana. In its short length lie several small bars which offer a variety of fine dishes, all neatly described and priced on cards for the customer to peruse. In one stands a stall of fresh seafood, stocked with crabs, and prawns of all sizes, from the large and expensive *langostinos* of Sanlúcar to the tiny *camarones*, no more than a half an inch long, which are eaten whole, washed down with cold beer. Another is a *freiduria*, a local speciality copied elsewhere with little success. Here one may see fish of all kinds crisply fried on the spot. The usual *calamares* and *boquerones* always appear, but there is one particular Cádiz creature which should be tried by the adventurous, the *choco*. This is a large white cuttlefish peculiar to the region, with a taste which is sweeter and less fishy than the common squid. Deep fried crab claws, tiny plates of paella, miniature shrimp omelettes, seafood kebabs, fine mountain ham and sausage... a complete meal may be had in Zorrilla in several different premises without walking more than a couple of hundred yards.

Lunch in Cádiz.

The enormous variety of local fish available to the Gadetano chef can be seen in the colourful main market which lies near the cathedral. As is customary in Spain, the more plentiful the produce the more frantic becomes the Spanish housewife to buy it before her near neighbour, so the morning sessions are hectic and amusing. Outside, gypsies sell different varieties of snails and herbs collected in the countryside, shoe menders try to drum up custom, and itinerant Moroccans attempt to interest all and sundry in cheap stereos, bad rugs and fake watches. In short, a fine example of modern Spanish market life, and an endless source of free entertainment for the visitor.

The cathedral is, inevitably, in a state of restoration, but visitable nevertheless. There is a rich treasury in which sumptuousness goes well beyond the bounds of good taste. It is a reflection of the wealth which Cádiz won through trade with the colonies of the New World. The most famous item is the 'million monstrance', a vast confection of silver and, reputedly, a million jewels which must be one of the most valuable hideous objects on earth. The term monstrance is an ecclesiastical one, from the Latin verb to show, not a comment on its aesthetic value. It is somewhat difficult to concentrate on the rest of the collection after meeting this particular nightmare. There are the usual saintly relics which should be treated with the scepticism they deserve – one does not need to be a mathematician to work out that the average Spanish saint clearly possessed six arms and an extraordinary wealth of internal organs beyond the comprehension of modern medicine.

The cathedral itself is vast and plain by comparison with this overblown display of ecclesiastical largesse. Its finest point is the quiet, domed crypt where the composer Manuel de Falla, one of the most famous Gadetanos of all, is buried. The rest of the city's sights are minor ones, and the visitor may prefer an aimless wander or an hour in the Parque Genovés, admiring the rare tropical plants and watching the fishermen.

The Oratory of La Santa Cueva, near the Plaza Mina in Francisco, has three works by Goya which are not of his best. It is an odd little place of worship, and to gain entrance you may well have to ask at a nearby café or shop for the caretaker. The church of San Felipe Neri, where the *Cortes* gathered in 1812 to proclaim the constitution, bears many plaques on its walls recording its historic past.

Overnight in Cádiz.

ACCOMMODATION

Hotel Atlántico
Duque de Nájera 9
Cádiz
Tel: 212301

If you cannot stay in the Atlántico then it may be as well to commute to Cádiz by the *Vapor* from El Puerto. This is a magnificent modern hotel, part of the parador chain, situated in gardens close to the Parque Genovés, overlooking the Atlantic. The rooms are quiet, the service of the very best. The Atlántico attracts return visitors by the score and advance booking is essential except in the depths of winter.

Open all year
Rooms: 153
Credit cards: American Express, Diner's Club, Eurocard, Visa
Rating ****

Francia y Paris
Plaza Calvo Sotelo 2
Cádiz
Tel: 212319

Inexpensive local accommodation in the heart of the city.

Open all year
Rooms: 69
Credit cards: American Express, Diner's Club, Eurocard, Visa
Rating **

EATING OUT

El Faro
San Félix 15
Cádiz
Tel: 211068

El Faro has the customary Gadetano skill with fish and some innovative ideas too. There are interesting dishes of *revueltos*, lightly scrambled eggs with salt cod (*bacalao*) or peppers and prawns, brains in sherry vinegar, and *sopa al cuarta de hora*, quarter hour soup, made from fish in 15 minutes.

Open every day
Credit cards: American Express, Diner's Club, Eurocard, Visa
Rating ****

El Anteojo
Alameda de Apodaca 22
Cádiz
Tel: 221320

Good paella, Galician octopus (*pulpo gallego*), cod roe (*huevos aliñadas*), and *choco* close to Zorrilla on the seafront.

Open every day
Credit cards: American Express, Diner's Club, Eurocard, Visa
Rating ***

CADIZ: USEFUL INFORMATION

Tourist office:	Calderón de la Barca, 1
	Tel: 211313
Population:	503,251
Facilities:	airport, bullring, passenger ferries to North Africa, and the Canary Islands

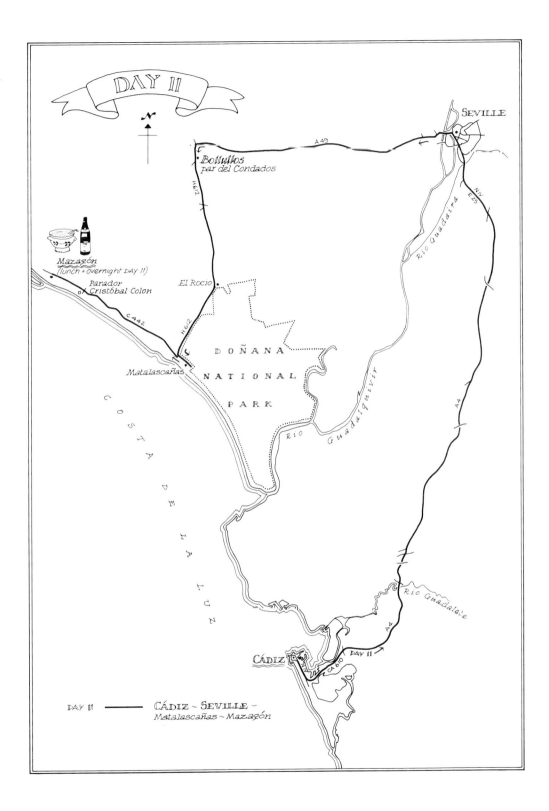

DAY 11

SEVILLE

A 49

Bollullos
par del Condados

H 612

NN

E 25

Rio Guadaira

Mazagón
(lunch + overnight DAY 11)

Parador
Cristóbal Colon

El Rocio

C 442

H 612

Matalascañas

D O Ñ A N A

N A T I O N A L

P A R K

Rio

Guadalquivir

A 4

C O S T A   D E   L A   L U Z

Rio Guadalaie

A 4

CÁDIZ

CA 610   DAY 11

DAY 11 ——— CÁDIZ ~ SEVILLE ~
Matalascañas ~ Mazagón

Church of San José, Cádiz

DAY 11

Cádiz to the Huelva coast and the park of Doñana, about 160 miles.

The longest drive of the journey brings the visitor back to Seville to travel around the great swamps of Las Marismas which form where the Guadalquivir meets the sea. Beyond Seville the route moves through the wine growing town of Bollullos par del Condado, El Rocio, scene of an annual pilgrimage by horse drawn carriage, and ends at the secluded coast by the national park of Doñana, where there is a modern parador in a forest by the sea.

Overnight in Mazagón.

Route shown p. 119.

Map references

Cádiz	36° 32´N 6° 18´W
Seville	37° 25´N 5° 58´W
Bollullos par del Condado	37° 20´N 6° 35´W
El Rocio	37° 08´N 6° 30´W
Matalascañas	37° 00´N 6° 32´W
Mazagón	37° 08´N 6° 50´W

Breakfast in Cádiz.

Las Marismas, the swamps of the Guadalquivir basin, divide the provinces of Cádiz and Huelva, an uncrossable and shifting territory that is one of the most important wildlife reserves in Europe. The private motor car is completely banned from the areas where the rarest wildlife lives. No major bridge or road has ever spanned the temperamental waters of the Guadalquivir after Seville which, like those of the Missisippi, change course and height from decade to decade.

Once, there were large islands in the Guadalquivir and, on a famous occasion, marauding Vikings on a southerly expedition captured one and settled there, making frequent forays to attack the Arab city of Seville. When they were finally overcome, they were offered the chance to become Moslems or die... and immediately switched their allegiance from Wotan to Allah, adding another racial strain to the heady mix which forms the faces of modern Andalucia. Fair hair is by no means uncommon here, and it is thought an asset in a female dancer.

The impasse created by Las Marismas means that the visitor who wants to explore the northern part of the Costa de la Luz must return to Seville and take the Huelva highway there. It is no great burden. From Cádiz runs a fast, toll motorway which links to a similar route running west of the city. There is little to see between Cádiz and Seville that has not already been mentioned. The motorway is barely used, even at the busiest times of year, making the journey easy and swift. The reasons for this obvious boycott are obscure. Perhaps the Spanish do not take to the idea of paying tolls. More likely, they miss the profusion of roadside bars and ventas which accompany every other route to provide refreshment for the traveller.

This is a country where the average lorry driver will consume an enormous quantity at any hour of the day. One such beefy chap I encountered on the road from Tarifa to Cádiz consumed, in the space of fifteen minutes, one black coffee, a large brandy, a beer and two toasted bread rolls liberally smothered from a big tub of pork dripping, flavoured with paprika and dyed bright red, the latter a popular alternative to butter and marmalade in these parts. And all this at seven in the morning... the motorways clearly have a lot of catching up to do.

Seville

Shortly before Seville there is a ring road signposted to Huelva, but it is hardly worth taking. If you carry straight on you are soon brought into the broad, palm-lined avenue of Las Palmeras which changes, imperceptibly, into Las Delicias as the Guadalquivir appears on the right, and finally becomes the Paseo Cristóbal Colón at the Torre del Oro as one sweeps past the familiar sights of central, riverside Seville. There are few grander entrances into a great city in Europe, and it would be a shame to miss it for the sake of a few minutes saved in driving time.

Follow the signs for the Huelva motorway after the Triana bridge. The fast motorway to the Portuguese border appears, accompanied for much of its length by the old N431, running through a series of towns of minor interest. They are best left for the moment, and seen on the return from Ayamonte. There is a fork onto a minor road to the coast, the H612, signposted for Bollullos par del Condado and El Rocio around 32 miles from Seville (take care not to confuse this with the earlier turning for Bollullos de la Mitacíon, an unobjectionable place, but the wrong one).

Bollullos par del Condado

The pace of life here is much quieter than in Cádiz or Seville, as may be judged from Bollullos, a rather dapper little spot which makes a tidy living from producing decent table wine. There is a handful of modest *bodegas* which give a friendly welcome to visitors – this is a far cry from the professional marketing of Jerez. There is no pretence that the wines of the area are anything but decent *vinos de la mesa*, and the quality varies greatly from *bodega* to *bodega*, and harvest to harvest. Whites, reds and *olorosos* are produced in quantity, as well as *mosto* which is drunk young, like Beaujolais Nouveau (though the vintners of Villefranche have little to lose sleep over).

El Rocio

Moving towards the coast, along the edges of the national park of Doñana, one reaches El Rocio, an unremarkable town until one is about to leave it and sees, on the left, a brilliant white church, with a scallop shell portal, gleaming by the waters of the swamp. This is the church of Nuestra Señora del Rocio, the object of devotion for the greatest annual romería in Spain.

Each Whitsuntide as many as a million Andalucians gather in the area to take part in festive romerías, of which that of El Rocio is the best known. They trek across the flat marshes, in costume, singing and dancing, in great moving droves of horse drawn carts, rather like the wagon trains of the old West.

It is typical of Spain that, while traditions such as these are dying through lack of interest in other countries, the romerías become ever more popular each year. The love of public ritual – at the romería, the feria, *Semana Santa* or the *corrida* – is an integral facet of the national character. The peak of the romería to El Rocio is the procession of the Virgin, carried through the streets by brotherhoods from different villages who almost come to blows over the right to support her.

Of course, no one sleeps a wink for days, and vast quantities of *fino* and *manzanilla* are consumed en route, but the devotion is real enough, as one can judge by the number of visitors to El Rocio during quieter times of the year. It is impossible for anyone who is not Spanish to fully appreciate, or participate in, these events. But if you are in the area when they are happening, take the advice of the tourist office in Seville, or that of your hotel reception about the practicalities of a visit. Bear in mind that the Spanish do not enter into these things half-heartedly, and the itinerary of a visitor who wants to spend an hour or so soaking up the atmosphere before moving on to the next parador might not fit in with that of a few hundred thousand people crossing the swamp in horse-drawn wagons.

The romería is strewn with souvenirs and mementoes for those who take part in it. One of the most illuminating, though you may not see it outside private homes, is a colour photograph of the man of the house, three days into the trip, wearing rough stubble, a *caballero* hat, and the misty-eyed expression of profound weariness copied directly from the hero of a spaghetti western. These portraits can be difficult to place; is this *macho* figure really the taxi driver or bank clerk who has just spruced himself up for work?

Matalascañas

The coast is reached at the modern resort of Matalascañas, populated almost entirely by domestic tourists. From here, running west to the border, lie endless golden beaches behind pine woods. They are little used, except at weekends in the summer when a large part of Seville descends for barbecues, beach parties, boy scout camps and nature rambles, a kind of romería dedicated to the god of the sun. It's an amiable, if occasionally hectic, experience.

Lunch at Mazagón.

It may be escaped in its entirety – except for Sunday lunch – by staying at the excellent modern Parador Cristóbal Colón, built by a pine forest near an excellent beach, halfway between Matalascañas and the small resort of Mazagón on the way to Huelva, which also happens to house the best restaurant in the area. I can think of only one quieter parador in Andalucia, and that is at the other end of the region, close to the source of the Guadalquivir in the Sierra de Cazorla.

Overnight in Mazagón.

ACCOMMODATION

Parador Cristóbal Colón
Mazagón-Moguer
Tel: 376000

A modern, secluded parador close to the beach and pine forest between the small tourist towns of Mazagón and Matalascañas. The rooms look out onto immaculate sub-tropical gardens, and there is a good swimming pool, though the beach is usually empty except at weekends. The restaurant is the only adventurous place to eat in the area; international and local dishes such as *pargo encebollado* (sea bream with onions) and *rape a la marinera* (monkfish in *marinera* sauce).

Open all year
Rooms: 20
Facilities: indoor pool, tennis, gardens
Credit cards: American Express, Diner's Club, Eurocard, Visa
Rating ***

Hosteleria de la Rábida
Paraje de la Rábida
La Rábida (seven miles from Mazagón)
Tel: 350312

Small, modern hostel in quiet gardens next to the monastery with a good restaurant, booked to capacity most Sundays. Booking is advisable.

Open all year
Rooms: 5
No credit cards
Rating **

EATING OUT

The best restaurant in the area is at the parador. There are modest seafood restaurants and tapas bars in Mazagón, Matalascañas and Bollullos.

EL ROCIO: USEFUL INFORMATION

The romería takes place each year during Whitsuntide weekend, beginning on the Saturday before the holiday. The Spanish National Tourist Office publishes an annual calendar of religious and other festivals, including El Rocio.
Its London office is 57/58 St James St,
London SW1A 1LD. Tel: 01-499-1169.

DONANA: USEFUL INFORMATION

The park is best visited in Spring. The Information Centre at La Rocina is open every day from 9.30am to 1.30pm, tel: (955) 406140. There are two four-hour guided excursions into the park daily, one in the morning and one in the afternoon. Departure times vary during the year. Seats must be booked in advance on (955) 430432, (955) 406140, or (954) 232230.

127

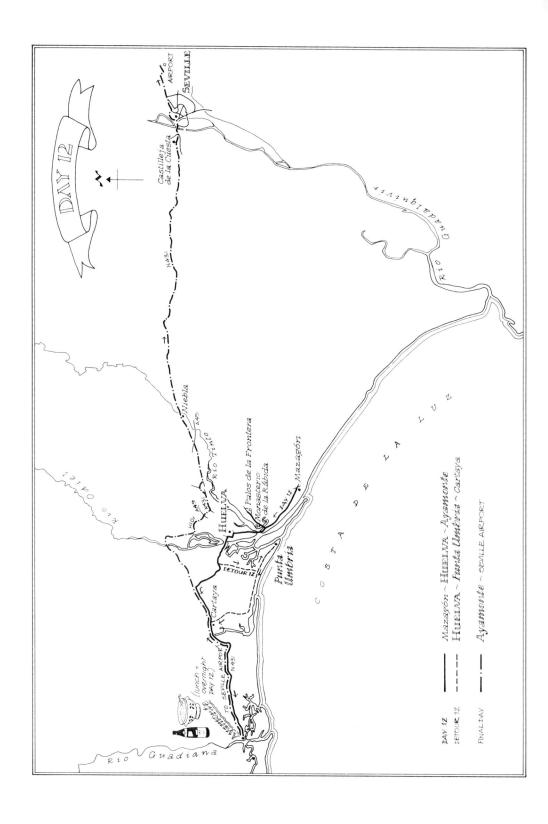

DAY 12

Castilleja de la Cuesta

SEVILLE

N431

Niebla

Rio Tinto

A49

N431

HUELVA

Palos de la Frontera
Monasterio
de la Rábida

Mazagón

Punta
Umbria

Rio Odiel

Cartaya

DETOUR 12

SEVILLE AIRPORT

Ayamonte
TO SEVILLE AIRPORT
N431

Lunch +
overnight
DAY 12

Rio Guadiana

C O S T A   D E   L A   L U Z

Rio Guadalquivir

DAY 12 ————————— Mazagón ~ Huelva ~ Ayamonte

DETOUR 12 ————————— Huelva ~ Punta Umbria ~ Cartaya

FINAL DAY ————————— Ayamonte ~ Seville Airport

DAY 12

From Mazagón to Ayamonte via the monastery of La Rábida and Huelva, about 65 miles.

The Monastery of La Rábida, which played an important part in the formation of Columbus's expedition to the New World, overlooks the regional capital of Huelva. From it, the route continues west, towards the Algarve, ending at the border town of Ayamonte where an excellent parador overlooks the river Guadiana, crossed by ferries between Spain and Portugal. From Ayamonte it is a direct route back to Seville, approx. 90 miles, and the airport.

Overnight at Ayamonte.

Map references
Mazagón	37° 08´N 6° 50´W
La Rábida	37° 12´N 6° 57´W
Palos de la Frontera	37° 13´N 6° 55´W
Huelva	37° 14´N 6° 58´W
Punta Umbria	37° 10´N 6° 59´W
Ayamonte	37° 14´N 7° 23´W
Niebla	37° 22´N 6° 41´W

Punta Umbria,

Breakfast in Mazagón.

Las Marismas once stretched unspoilt from the mouth of the Guadalquivir to the provincial capital of Huelva. Over the last century, Huelva has turned into an industrial port of some size, and its ancillary workings have spread somewhat to the south, bringing vast sugar plants and chemical wharfs onto the flat swamp land. The industrialisation of Huelva was largely begun by a famous British name, Rio Tinto Zinc, the Tinto being one of the two rivers which converge at the town. The vast, open-cast ore mines of RTZ near Nerva to the north are now a tourist attraction for those fascinated by the mining process; the area also has several estates of very English looking bungalows, built for the executives uprooted from Surrey and points north to run the operation. The mining of pyrites in the area goes back to Roman times.

Travelling from Mazagón towards Huelva, one is puzzled to see, amid all this growing commerce, signs indicating the Ruta Colombina, the route of Columbus. But this area is at the very heart of the Columbus story, and some of its most important episodes were played out along this stretch of Atlantic sand. Before Huelva a right turn leads to the small monastery of La Rábida, on a hill overlooking the joining of the Tinto and Odiel rivers. Below is an enormous statue of Columbus by the American sculptor Gertrude Whitney, looking out to sea and the New World he discovered.

La Rábida

Without the intervention of the fathers of this small monastery, it is doubtful that he would ever have made the journey... at least under the Spanish flag. There is no space here to tell the Columbus story in anything but the briefest detail. It is, in any case, one of those tales of history in which it is extremely difficult to separate fact from fiction. We do know with some certainty, however, that the Spanish monarchs Ferdinand and Isabel were unimpressed by Columbus's plans when he first presented them. This is often interpreted as short-sightedness on their part; it should be remembered that, at the time, Ferdinand and Isabel were on the verge of completing the Christian Reconquest of Spain with the final battle against Granada, ending a campaign which had begun nearly three centuries earlier. The pleas of a strange, white-haired foreign sea captain for hefty sums

131

to finance an uncertain expedition to discover a new route to the east may not have been at the front of their minds.

Columbus visited the monastery of La Rábida, stayed there and told the fathers of his plans. Impressed, they took up his cause with local men of influence and the persistent navigator finally won through. Had Isabel not relented, it seems certain that Columbus would have gone elsewhere for backing, and perhaps made the journey under the patronage of the English or French crowns – since he was, himself, a Genoan, national pride would have played no part in his decision.

The little monastery would make an interesting visit even without the Columbus connections. It is in a picturesque location, with fine gardens and parks running down the hill. Models of the three caravels which set sail from nearby Palos de la Frontera, the study where Columbus is reputed to have worked, and other objects of Colombiana are in its possession. The building is early 14th century and is an attractive example of *mudéjar* work carried out on a small scale. There is a hostel with a good restaurant virtually next to the monastery.

Palos de la Frontera

Palos de la Frontera, two miles away, is the port where the three caravels set sail. While this may be a matter of local pride today, one wonders what the townsfolk felt at the time when they were ordered to select from among them some of the crews for the little fleet bound for an uncertain destination. The local tourist guides refer to the 'enrolment' of the men from the steps of the Church of San Jorge; the truth was closer to press-ganging. The church is now preserved as a national monument.

Huelva

Huelva has nothing to offer the visitor except the usual handful of good fish taverns around the centre of the town. There are two possible routes to the end of the Costa de la Luz – and of the Spanish coast itself. The slower is via Punta Umbria, a popular summer beach resort for domestic holidaymakers which lies on the promontory opposite Huelva to which it is linked by a pleasant boat service. From Punta Umbria the minor road moves inland to Cartaya where it joins the main N431 highway which provides the alternative, faster route east. The main road is just as pleasant, running through fragrant, fruit-growing land, perfumed by thyme, fir and orange blossom, with strawberry, raspberry and fig fields by the side of the road. One is reminded of the Algarve of old, just across the border, and the odd solitary villa possesses a familiar Portuguese chimney. The food is, of course, immeasurably better, nor is there the rash of thoughtless development which is marring the coast from Villa Real to well beyond Faro.

Ayamonte

There is nothing of a cultural nature to see, but then it does strike me that it is as well to finish a tour of Spain in circumstances where no galleries, museums or churches are beckoning at one's elbow. As I said in Seville at the start of the journey, this is a rich feast to digest, and at its close there is, for most of us, nothing more pleasant than to be in quiet surroundings, preferably by the sea. In Ayamonte the signs for the parador lead to a hill which stands over the brilliant white town. One can see across the river Guadiana, which marks the border, to Villa Real and beyond, north into the sleepy agricultural land on either side of the river, and back along the Costa de la Luz, where miles of largely unoccupied golden beaches stretch to the small fishing town of Isla Cristina.

Lunch in Ayamonte.

The modern little parador is a delight, with a restaurant serving local specialities like skate with red pepper, but there is little of moment to see in the town. The brief trip across the river into Portugal is inexpensive and pleasant; the only item worth buying there is, naturally, port.

Overnight at Ayamonte.

Return to Seville.

After spending your last evening at Ayamonte, the route returns to Seville, 90 miles to the east. On the return journey, the traveller with time should use the old N431 instead of the motorway, for there are two worthwhile stops.

Niebla, ten miles after Huelva, is a picturesque hill town with Arab walls, a Roman bridge, and a handsome church with Moslem antecedents. Castilleja de la Cuesta, now virtually a suburb of Seville, houses the convent where the explorer Cortés died, but is much better known in the city as the source of some of the best pastries in Andalucia, a personal favourite being the *torta de aceite*, a crispy thin biscuit wrapped in greased paper. Many more sophisticated pastries are on show in the town bakeries, and welcome presents they make too if one can eventually bear to part with them.

Not one of Castilleja's delightful cakes tastes a mite as delicious at home as it does in a Seville café, a steaming glass of *solo* on the counter, the chatter of gossiping locals and the cries of the lottery ticket merchants echoing around the walls, the smell of southern Spain, hot and exotic on the air.

ACCOMMODATION

Parador Costa de la Luz
El Castillito
Ayamonte
Tel: 320700

Modern parador with scenic location on a hill overlooking Ayamonte. Comfortable rooms compatible with its three-star parador rating – most paradors are four star. Probably the best restaurant in the area, with local and international dishes.

Open all year
Rooms: 20
Credit cards: American Express, Diner's Club, Eurocard, Visa
Rating ***

EATING OUT

Casa Barberi
Paseo de la Ribera
Ayamonte
Tel: 320298

Popular local restaurant with terrace on the road to the port. Conventional Spanish fish dishes, prawns, hake, and the local skate when available.

Closed Tuesdays and January
Credit cards: American Express, Diner's Club, Visa
Rating **

HUELVA: USEFUL INFORMATION	
Tourist office:	Fernando el Católico 18
	Tel: 277467/258467
Population:	135,000

Recipes
from the Region

MENU 1

Gazpacho
Cold Andalucian soup

. . .

Rabos de toro
Oxtails

. . .

Helado Moscatel
Muscatel ice cream

Gazpacho
Cold Andalucian soup

2 green peppers
4 beef tomatoes
2 slices bread
1/2 cucumber
1/2 onion
1 clove garlic
5 tbsp olive oil
2 tbsp wine vinegar
1 pt/600ml water
salt to taste
Garnish: croutons,
finely chopped onion,
tomato and cucumber

Serves 4

There is no single recipe for gazpacho. Every household likes its own proportions of ingredients, and the soup lends itself to improvisation with other fresh salad vegetables such as avocado. Freshness is the very essence of gazpacho. If made with tired ingredients, then the results, inevitably, are disappointing.

Gazpacho is a versatile invention, and can even be found served in glasses with ice and a slug of vodka as a kind of Spanish Bloody Mary.

Traditionally, the soup was made with a pestle and mortar, and there are still those who say that no other form of preparation yields better results. Personally, I find a food processor preferable to the tedious pounding required when working by hand.

Remove the crusts of the bread and soak in water. Peel and chop the tomatoes, garlic and other vegetables and liquidise until they are a fine purée. Pour most of the mixture into a bowl. Squeeze the bread and liquidise it with the remaining vegetable purée. Slowly add the salt and oil, followed by the vinegar. Mix with the soup in the bowl and adjust the seasoning.

Separately serve a bowl of croutons and finely chopped onion, cucumber and tomatoes to be sprinkled on the soup.

Rabos de toro
Oxtails

4 lb/2 kg oxtails
(about four tails)
2 lb/1kg onions
1 lb/500g tomatoes
4 cloves of garlic
1/2 bottle dry sherry or
wine
salt and pepper

Serves 4

This is a favourite dish in Seville, in modest restaurants and more famous ones such as the Burladero.

Trim all the fat from the oxtails and fry the chopped onions until they are golden. Remove the onions, then brown the tails and return the onions with the chopped tomatoes and seasoning, stirring the oxtails to absorb the mixture.

Add the wine and cook slowly, covered, for around three hours (45 minutes in a pressure cooker). Test to ensure the meat is cooked.

Oxtails should never be served fresh from the pan. Once cooked, drain and allow them to cool for at least two hours then reheat in a frying pan with olive oil. Use the well-cooked vegetables in the pan as a garnish for the dish; the juice makes lovely stock for soup.

Helado Moscatel
Muscatel ice cream

sufficient ice cream for
four people (about
1lb/500g)
a handful of raisins
Málaga or other sweet
wine

Serves 4

Use good quality plain ice cream – the flavour known as *nata*, literally cream, is used in Spain. Superior vanilla dairy cream is the best alternative elsewhere.

Blend the softened ice cream with the raisins and serve with a dash of Málaga or other sweet wine.

MENU 2

Caldo de perro
'Dog soup'

. . .

Urta a la Roteña
Bream, Rota style

. . .

Manzanas Rellenas
Stuffed apples

Caldo de perro
'Dog soup'

1 lb/500g white fish,
filleted
2 pt/1.2l water or fish
stock
1 onion
1 green pepper
1 bitter orange or 1
orange and 1 lemon
4 tbsp olive oil
1 clove garlic, chopped
seasoning

Serves 4

'Dog soup' is a speciality of Cádiz, a city which is also fond of 'Cat soup'. Neither is what it seems; the former being a fish soup made with the juice of bitter, marmalade oranges, and the latter a variation on the popular hot garlic soup, *sopa de ajo*. 'Cádiz fish soup' might make a better description of this excellent starter for guests with whom one is only on nodding relations.

Brown the chopped garlic in the oil with the chopped green pepper and onion, then add the water or stock. Simmer, covered, for 10 minutes then add the fish pieces. Peel the orange and add the chopped skin and juice to the soup. Season and serve when the fish is cooked, about eight minutes after it is placed in the pan.

Urta a la Roteña
Bream, Rota style

2 lb/1kg white fish
1 onion
3 green peppers
1 tomato
flour
1/2 bottle white wine
2 tbsp brandy
olive oil
salt and pepper

Serves 4

This a common dish throughout the Costa de la Luz. *Urta* is a variety of sea bream. Any firm seafish, such as cod, turbot or halibut can be substituted.

Brown the chopped onion, tomato and peppers in oil on a high heat in a frying pan. When they are beginning to soften, add the white wine and seasonings and leave to cook for 10 minutes.

143

Cut the fish into thick slices, removing the central bone if possible. Coat with flour and brown in olive oil. Heat the brandy and flame the fish in the pan, then turn down the heat to keep the fish cooking gently. Add the vegetable broth to the fish pan, and simmer gently until the fish is cooked, which will usually take a further 10 minutes.

Manzanas Rellenas
Stuffed Apples

4 apples
4 oz/125g walnuts
6 oz/175g dates or figs
$1/3$ bottle sweet sherry
or wine
2 oz/60g sugar

Serves 4

Crush the walnut kernels and mix with the chopped dates or figs. Core the apples and stuff with the date mixture. Place in a baking dish and pour the sherry around the apples. If necessary, top up with water so that liquid covers about a third of the apples. Sprinkle the fruit with sugar then cook in a medium oven for around 35 minutes or until the fruit is soft.

MENU 3

Escabeche de pescado
Cold marinated fish

. . .

Pato a la sevillana
Duck, Seville style

. . .

Melocotón con vino
Peaches with wine

Escabeche de pescado
Cold marinated fish

4 medium-sized
herrings or mackerel
$1/2$ pt/300ml wine
vinegar
$1/4$ pt/150ml water
$1/3$ bottle white wine or
dry sherry
4 bay leaves
10 peppercorns
10 coriander seeds
(optional)
pinch of sugar
2 red peppers
1 onion

Serves 4

Prepare at least 24 hours in advance.

There are many variations on the theme of cold,
marinated fish, a dish which is a close relation to
that old British favourite, soused herring. Garlic,
thyme, paprika and oregano can be added to the
flavourings, and the amount of sugar varies
according to taste – commercial varieties always
being on the sweet side.

Bring the vinegar, water, wine and flavourings to a
gentle boil and leave, covered, simmering for 10
minutes. Fillet the fish and brown briefly in hot
oil then place in a shallow oven dish wide enough
to hold the four fish. Sear the chopped red peppers in the frying pan and slice the onion.

Cover the fish fillets with peppers and onion slices
then pour on the liquid. Cover the oven dish with
foil and cook for 30 minutes in a medium oven.
Allow to cool then chill, covered with film. The
flavours will have spread throughout the dish
within 24 hours, but the fish will keep for up to
four days in a refrigerator.

146

Pato a la sevillana
Duck, Seville style

2 ducks
1 onion, sliced
1/2 bottle dry sherry or dry white wine
1 tbsp flour
1 orange, preferably bitter
2 carrots
1 bay leaf
olive oil
salt and pepper
4 oz/125g green olives

Serves 4

Best prepared 24 hours in advance.

Duck with olives is Seville's best-known regional dish, and one that is popular throughout Spain.

Depending on the size of the birds – and your casserole – quarter or halve the ducks. Brown with the sliced onion in the casserole in hot oil then remove and pour off most of the fat. Add the flour to the pan, allow to brown, then slowly add the sherry, stirring to prevent the formation of lumps.

Place the duck pieces back in the casserole with the unskinned sliced orange, sliced carrots , bay leaf and seasonings, and add enough water to cover three quarters of the duck. Cook in a medium to hot oven for 90 minutes checking that the meat is cooked. Add the chopped olives at the end of the cooking period.

The dish can be served immediately, after being skimmed for fat. Alternatively, allow to cool, remove the congealed fat the next day, then reheat.

Melocotón con vino
Peaches with wine

8 ripe peaches or
nectarines
$1/2$ bottle red wine
2 oz/50g sugar
1 stick cinnamon
a wine glass of brandy

Serves 4

Prepare 4 days in advance.

Gently heat all ingredients except the peaches in
a pan until the sugar is dissolved. Then pour the
mixture over the washed, sliced fruit in a serving
bowl.

Cover with film and keep chilled until an hour
before serving.

Glossary of Food Terms

Starters (Entreméses)

arroz brut	dry soup of rice and various meats
arroz marinera	light, saffron and rice soup
boquerones	anchovies, usually in vinegar
croquetas	plain, breadcrumbed chicken croquettes
ensalada de pimientos asados	roast pepper salad
entreméses variados	variety of cooked meats and salads
esparragos	asparagus
flamenquines	ham and cheese rolls, fried
gazpacho	cold soup of tomatoes, peppers, garlic and onion
mejillónes marinara	mussels in strong tomato stock
salpicon de mariscos	seafood cocktail
sopa de ajo	garlic soup
sopa de almendras	filling, hot almond soup
sopa de tomate	local, garlic-flavoured tomato soup

Meats (Carne)

bistec	beefsteak
buey	ox
butifarra	spiced pork sausage
cabrito	kid
carnero	mutton
cerdo	pork
chorizo	highly spiced pork sausage
choto	mountain kid
cordero	lamb
frito	fried offal and vegetables
jamón	ham
pincho	seasoned kebab
sesos	brains
solomillo	sirloin steak
ternera	veal, beef

Poultry and Game (Ave y Caza)

codorniz	quail
conejo	rabbit

jabilí	wild boar
liebre	hare
pato	duck
pavo	turkey
pcrdiz	partridge
pintada	guinea fowl
pollo	chicken
tordo	thrush
venado	venison

Fish (Pescado)

anchoa	anchovy
anguila	eel
atún	tuna
bacalao	salt cod
besugo	sea bream
cazón	dogfish
chanquete	whitebait
dorada	gilthead
emperador (pez espada)	swordfish
lenguado	sole
lubina	sea bass
merluza	hake
parrillada	grilled selection of fish
rape	monkfish
rodaballo	turbot
salmonete	red mullet
salmón	salmon
sardina	sardine
trucha	trout

Seafood (Mariscos)

almeja	clam
berberecho	cockle
buey de mar	northern crab
calamar	squid
camarón	shrimp
cangrejo	crab

151

Seville

centolla	spider crab
chipirón	small squid
choco	large squid, normally from Cádiz
concha fina	Venus clam
cigala	large variety of prawn
gamba	prawn
langosta	lobster
langostino	Dublin Bay prawn
mejillón	mussel
ostra	oyster
percebe	barnacle
pulpo	octopus
sepia	cuttlefish

Vegetables (Verduras)

aguacete	avocado
ajo	garlic
alcachofa	artichoke
alcaparra	caper
berenjena	aubergine
cebolla	onion
champiñones	mushrooms
coliflor	cauliflower
endivas	endives
espárragos	asparagus
garbanzos	chick peas
guisantes	peas
habas	dried broad beans
judías	green beans
lechuga	lettuce
lombarda	red cabbage
patatas	potatoes
pepinillo	cucumber
pimiento	pepper
remolacha	beetroot
seta	wild mushroom
tomate	tomato
verdura	greens
zanahoria	carrot

Fruit (Fruta)

albaricoque	apricot
cereza	cherry
ciruela	plum
clementina	mandarin orange
fresa	strawberry
granada	pomegranate
higo	fig
lima	lime
limón	lemon
manzana	apple
melocotón	peach
melón	melon
membrillo	quince
naranja	orange
pera	pear
plátano	banana
uva	grape

Selected Bibliography

South from Granada, Gerald Brenan, Cambridge University Press, 1981. Brenan's best-known work in English documents life in the Alpujarra in the 1930s.

The Foods and Wines of Spain, Penelope Casas, Penguin, 1985. Weighty and comprehensive handbook of traditional recipes and wine lore written by the American wife of an expatriate Spaniard.

LookOut, LookOut Publications, Puebla Lucia, 29640 Fuengirola (Málaga), Spain. Published monthly, *LookOut* is a superb English language magazine guide to the many facets of modern Spain, from life in the resorts to out-of-the-way places to visit. Useful restaurant reviews with an emphasis on the Costa del Sol. Essential for any regular visitor to Spain.

Iberia, James Michener, Random House, 1968. As one would expect of Michener, this vast and highly readable panorama attempts to cover every aspect of the Spanish character and nation... and almost succeeds. Somewhat dated, but widely available in paperback.

Spain, Jan Morris, Penguin, 1982. Well-travelled foreign correspondent turns her attention to the character and culture of modern Spain.

Cooking in Spain, Janet Mendel Searl, LookOut Publications, Spain, 1987. Unquestionably the best English language guide to Spanish cooking currently available. In addition to hundreds of recipes, the author translates virtually every possible ingredient of Spanish dishes and offers advice on selecting wines and buying everyday food in local markets. Invaluable and, at 400 pages for under £5, excellent value.

Geographical Index

Recipe Index